A Leader's Guide to

MANAGING TRANSITIONS
FOR TEENS

By Youth Communication

By Youth Communication

Read. Write. Succeed.

A Leader's Guide to
MAGAGING TRANSITIONS
FOR TEENS
MAKING THE MOST OF CHANGE

Executive Editors
Laura Longhine and Keith Hefner

Principal Writer
Autumn Spanne

Contributing Writers and Workshop Leaders
Rachel Blustain, Laura Longhine, Nora McCarthy, Autumn Spanne

Layout & Design
Efrain Reyes, Jr. and Stephanie Liu

Cover
Adapted from Alex Camlin's cover design for *Managing Transitions*, by William Bridges

For reprint information, please contact Youth Communication.

ISBN 978-1-935552-71-0

First Edition

Printed in the United States of America

Youth Communication °
New York, New York
www.youthcomm.org

Acknowledgments

The development, testing, and writing of this curriculum was generously supported by the **Andrus Foundation**, which introduced us to the Transitions Framework. Thank you to Andrus staff and consultants who helped guide the project and provided feedback: Roger Conner, Vaughn Crandall, Steve Kelban, and Masiel Rodriguez-Vars.

Several dozen teens at Youth Communication participated in the workshops in which this material was tested and developed. They provided advice and feedback that shaped this material in every way. We would particularly like to thank the following teens:

Miguel Ayala
Yuhanna Buggs
Samantha Flowers
Armando Goodwin
Pauline Gordon
Erica Harrigan
Gilbert Howard

Lonnie Macloed
Cynthia Orbes
Michael Orr
Hattie Rice
Manny Sanchez
Natasha Santos
Samantha Yang

William Bridges

This book relies entirely on *Managing Transitions* by William Bridges for its insights into change and transitions. However, we have been liberal in adapting his work to suit the needs of teens in foster care. For example, Mr. Bridges calls the stages of transitions "Endings," "the Neutral Zone," and "New Beginning." The teens in our program used "Letting Go," "Chaos," and "New Start," as the labels for the stages. We have made many other changes because they worked with the teens in our program. However, in some cases we may have strayed far from the model. While we are deeply grateful to Mr. Bridges, we are solely responsible for any changes and adaptations.

For more information and further reading: *Managing Transitions* is a brief and straightforward book. It includes much more about the Transitions Framework, including lots of helpful insights and strategies that we could not include in *Managing Transitions for Teens*. While it is not essential, if you are implementing this program with teens, we strongly encourage you to read *Managing Transitions*.

Table of Contents

Introduction to the Managing Transitions for Teens Program

PART I: Learning About Transitions

PART II: Transitions in Action

APPENDIX

Introduction to the
MANAGING TRANSITIONS
FOR TEENS
Program

Curriculum Planner—16 Sessions

Part I—Learning About Transitions

SESSION 1 **Welcome!** **Introduction to** **Transitions**	SESSION 2 **Building a Safe and** **Supportive Group**	SESSION 3 **Introducing the** **Tools**	SESSION 4 **Owning the Tools**
SESSION 5 **Stages of** **Transition—** **Letting Go**	SESSION 6 **Stages of** **Transition—** **Chaos**	SESSION 7 **Stages of** **Transition—** **New Start**	

Part II—Transitions in Action

SESSION 8 **Identifying Your** **Change**	SESSION 9 **Planning Out the** **Tools**	SESSION 10 **Using the Tools**	SESSION 11 **Using the Tools**
SESSION 2 **Using the Tools**	SESSION 13 **Using the Tools**	SESSION 14 **Using the Tools**	SESSION 15 **Using the Tools**
SESSION 16 **Celebration**			

Progress Is a Process:
A Step-by-Step Approach to Change and Transition

By Natasha Santos, teen workshop participant

Since 1993, when Youth Communication founded *Represent*, a magazine by and for youth in foster care, hundreds of our teen writers have made the transition to adult life (I'm one of them!). But we've noticed that even those of us who start out strong, with apartments, mentors, and other support, often feel like we're caught in a cyclone when we leave the system.

Every change—like starting a new job, or moving in with someone new—is accompanied by strong feelings. We feel anxiety about all the decisions we must make. We feel sadness, anger, and even a sense of abandonment at losing the security and stability of care without having family to turn to (no matter how much we disliked being in care). And we have fears about whether we'll be able to achieve our dreams (or just avoid becoming homeless!).

It's hard to know what might help us through the swirl of changes. How can you really teach young people to handle such unbelievably stressful circumstances? We've all been in "independent living" classes—and for many of us, they didn't help much.

Why We Created the Transitions Program

When the adult staff at Youth Communication heard about the "Transitions Framework" that is used by business managers to help employees adjust to changes on the job, they were intrigued. The framework, which is described by business guru William Bridges in his best-selling book *Managing Transitions*, lays out a step-by-step approach to managing the transitions in our lives.

Even in the hard business world, Bridges focuses on the emotional components that come with change.

His framework describes three stages of transition that will make sense to anyone who has ever been in foster care:

1. A time to acknowledge what you're losing and say goodbye.

2. A chaotic time of adjusting to the change when nothing feels familiar or solid but new possibilities are also wide open.

3. A time when the change begins to feel comfortable, especially when we are working toward new goals.

With each stage, there are strategies we can use that make the transition smoother, either by helping us face what we're losing, providing more structure to our days during a period of chaos, or celebrating our new start.

The Andrus Foundation thought the framework could help youth in foster care learn new strategies for managing the emotional transitions that come with change. We thought so too. Over a three-year period, Youth Communication ran several workshops and worked with individual teens to help us use the transition concepts and tools to cope with changes in our lives, whether changes we chose, or changes that were imposed on us. We saw real progress.

In this manual we've included the basics you'll need to run your own Transitions workshop with teens. It includes tons of lessons that help teens really feel and experience the transitions concepts. The lessons help young people understand the ideas by practicing them. It's a strategy that assumes that people learn best by doing. And besides, the goal of this program is that young people actually implement the transitions tools in their own lives, not just understand them. That way, teens can "survive the cyclone" and make a successful transition to adulthood. I know that's their goal, and I know that it's your goal too if you work with teens.

About me: I've made many transitions since participating in my first Transitions workshop. I graduated from high school in New York City, volunteered in New Orleans after Hurricane Katrina, attended college at the University of New Orleans, and participated in the Foster Club All Stars program. I still struggle, like everyone, but I'm doing so more successfully as a result of learning skills to manage the transitions in my life.

What Is the Transitions Program?

The program consists of this Leader's Guide and a Teen Journal. Youth Communication also offers training in how to use the materials.

The Leader's Guide: That's this book. It has lessons for 16 weeks of workshops that you can run with teens. (See a week-by-week calendar on p. 4.) The workshops are divided into two parts.

Part One begins with activities that focus on building trust in the group and easing into the concepts. Then it gets specific about the tools teens can use to manage transitions in their lives. In Part Two (weeks 8-16), every teen picks a change they want to address and then works on it for six weeks. They meet weekly to talk about their progress and to get feedback and support from the group (and from you, the facilitator).

The Teen Journal includes worksheets and stories that teens will need to participate in the program. You'll need one copy of the Journal for your own reference. In addition, each teen in your group should have his or her own journal. It will help them be active participants in the workshop. They'll complete activities that will help them learn about themselves and their strengths, and how to mobilize their strengths to manage transitions successfully.

When teens have completed the program, the journal will be a record of their accomplishments. It will also serve as a template for handling future changes—on the job, in relationships, and in other aspects of their lives.

Training: Youth Communication can offer training to your staff in how to implement the *Managing Transitions for Teens* program. Training can range from phone consultation to half- or full-day workshops at your site. For more information, contact Loretta Chan (lchan@youthcomm.org).

Who Should Lead These Workshops?

It's important that the workshops in this program be led by a trained professional—a social worker, psychologist, or caseworker who has experience working with teens in groups on sensitive topics.

Change is hard. It can be especially hard for youth who have been in foster care. To them, change is often associated with abandonment, betrayal, danger, and vulnerability. When faced with change, they may shut down, or act out. The goal of this program is to help young people become more effective at managing their responses to changes in their lives. But to reach that goal requires revisiting some changes from the past and practicing new responses to change.

While testing these lessons with teens, we found that going through that process inevitably brought up some raw emotions and painful memories. Teens will process these feelings in many different ways—feeling sad or depressed, acting out, skipping sessions, wondering if they should be in the workshop, projecting their feelings onto the adults or other teens in the group, etc. It's important that the group leader have some experience in managing these kinds of reactions.

Furthermore, in all of the groups that we ran while developing these lessons, we used two staff members. The second staff member does not need to be as skilled as the group leader. However, merely having two adults in the room at all times makes a big difference. You'll each notice different things, and you'll be able to compare notes after each session. That reduces stress on the adults and helps you to process any secondary trauma you may feel from the teens' revelations and struggles.

Finally, it is important to keep the adult-to-teen ratio low so you can respond thoroughly and supportively to the issues the teens raise. For two adults, a group of six to 10 teens is ideal. If the group grows beyond 10, we suggest adding a third staff member. And if the group grows much larger than 12 youth, we recommend splitting it into two groups, with two staff each. A big element in the success of this workshop will be the trust that develops among the participants, and it is easier to build that trust in a smaller group.

Who Should Participate?

Managing Transitions for Teens is designed for youth ages 15 to 20. We designed the program with youth in foster care in mind—and the struggles they will face when they leave the system to live on their own. However, this program could also be used with youth who are leaving juvenile justice systems, or making other difficult changes in their lives.

The workshop does not require strong academic skills, though teens will need reading skills at about the 4th grade level or above to read the stories and worksheets. It helps to have a few teens in the group with good conceptual skills who can get a solid grasp of the idea of the stages of transition. *But the real understanding of the concepts comes through the activities, not the reading.*

Throughout the program we refer to the participants interchangeably as teens (though some may be older), students (though some may not be in school), and youth.

Why Use Stories by Teens?

The most powerful influence on adolescents is their peers. They turn to each other for advice on everything from fashion to relationships to how to cope with traumatic events. But peer advice raises two challenges. The first is that much of it occurs outside of adult knowledge or supervision. Teens don't generally share their struggles with adults, especially not in adult-led group discussions. In addition, the quality of peer advice is mixed. There is a good reason why peer pressure—though it can sometimes be constructive—has a decidedly negative reputation.

Youth Communication's true stories by teens (and the activities that accompany them) help address both of those challenges. The stories have been carefully edited to insure that they include accurate information and show teens taking effective and appropriate action to learn new skills, develop more constructive attitudes, and manage the challenges in their lives.

The stories also work well because talking about the issues in the stories can be a safe way to introduce emotional topics. Discussing a story by a peer allows for some personal distance. This approach allows students to wrestle with important issues without having to delve into their own stories too soon. At the same time, because the writers are honest about difficult emotions and situations, the stories give teens permission to open up about their own experiences and feelings.

In this program, we use stories by teens to introduce the Transitions concepts and to show what different stages of transition look like in real life. In some of the lessons, and in the appendix, we provide journals from some of our teen workshop participants that document their journey through the program. These can be particularly helpful as a way of showing your group that other teens have struggled through this process, and learned from it.

Recruitment

We ran all of our Transitions programs as optional workshops. Teens had to apply, be accepted, and commit to participating in the full workshop. In return, they received a small stipend, as well as the opportunity to learn how to deal with change better and to work on managing a transition related to change they were struggling with in their own lives. Running the workshops this way enabled us to work with groups of teens who had committed to making changes in their lives and were motivated to do the hard work the program required. We recommend making your Transitions workshop optional if at all possible.

However, even if you are running your Transitions workshop as a mandatory activity, we strongly urge you to require all participants to complete an application. The application we provide here (on pp. 11-12) asks students to write about changes in their lives, and to explain what they hope to get out of the workshop and any questions or concerns they have. You can simply copy this application or adapt it to meet your needs. The application is important for two reasons:

1) It gives teens a sense of what the workshop will be about, and sends the signal that the program is serious—you'll be asking them to think deeply about their lives.

2) It gives you, the facilitator, a chance to start becoming familiar with the issues your teens may be bringing to the workshop, and what change they may eventually want to work on in the group.

After teens complete the application, it's a good idea to schedule interviews with each teen if possible—even if all of the teens will be accepted. This is a chance for you to talk with teens in more detail about the changes they've written about, clarify their goals for the workshop, and answer any questions they have about what to expect.

Attendance

As any experienced group leader knows, attendance can make or break a group. Because the Transitions workshop is long (16 sessions) and can be emotionally challenging, attendance can be an issue for even the most motivated teens. The application and interview process we've described above should help with this. Here are some other strategies:

• If possible, provide a small stipend or other reward to teens for completing the workshop with full participation.

• Make sure you have clear guidelines on attendance, lateness, and participation. Communicate these to your group before the workshop begins, and enforce them consistently.

• Take advantage of the power of the group. This curriculum includes lots of activities to build trust and a sense of ownership within the group, including having participants create their own group guidelines. Use this sense of mutual responsibility to reinforce the importance of attendance and participation—when some people miss sessions, it hurts the group as a whole. It's also important to praise good attendance and get group members to acknowledge each other when they are present. Address any attendance issues, and possible solutions, directly with the group

• Finally, pay close attention to how each participant is handling the emotional content of the workshop. Often, lateness and skipped sessions are symptoms of teens feeling anxious or overwhelmed by the content of the workshop. Take the time to meet privately with any students who are missing sessions, and try to address any concerns they may have.

TRANSITIONS WORKSHOP APPLICATION

Name _____

Best ways to contact you (phone, email, etc) _____

_____

PART 1: Identifying Changes/Transitions

Please write about three changes in your life:

1) A change that you feel you handled well

2) A change you're still going through that has been rough for you

3) A change you expect to happen in the near future that you're concerned about

Examples of changes might be: moving to a new foster home, changing schools, graduating high school, ending a friendship or other relationship, making a new friend, starting a new job, etc.

Write a few sentences (or more, if you like) about each change. Describe why you had to or decided to make the change. What were the main emotions you felt? What did you do to handle it? What was hard about it? What good things came out of it?

1) A change that you feel you handled well:

_____

_____

_____

_____

_____

_____

_____

_____

2) A change you're still going through that has been rough for you:

_____

_____

_____

(over)

_____

_____

_____

_____

_____

_____

3) A change you expect to happen in the near future that you're concerned about:

_____

_____

_____

_____

_____

_____

_____

_____

PART 2: Why You Want to Join the Workshop

Please describe why you would like to be part of the Transitions workshop. What do you hope to get out of it? What are your goals? What concerns or questions do you have?

_____

_____

_____

_____

_____

_____

_____

_____

_____

_____

_____

_____

How to Use This Book and the Lessons

The Leader's Guide contains complete instructions for facilitating all of the workshops in the *Managing Transitions for Teens* program. All of the workshops follow this format:

- Opening icebreaker/check-in

- Activity sessions/group discussion

- Closing reflection.

Before you meet with the teens:

1) Review the workshop summary

This will give you a quick overview of the focus of each workshop, including the youth development goals. You may want to write these goals on the board and mention them to the group at the beginning of each session.

2) Review the activities and worksheets; read the story (if there is one)

Review each activity in advance and imagine how your group will respond. For example, are they enthusiastic or shy about performing role plays? Are there participants who should not be in the same small group? Any thought you can give to the best way to organize the activities will be helpful.

If possible, complete the worksheets (which are in the Teen Journal) on your own so you will know what students may be feeling as they work on them. Also, if there's a story, read the story aloud to yourself so you'll have a feel for how it sounds and whether there are points that may be difficult or confusing for your teens.

3) Check to be sure you have the materials

Most of the lessons require only basic classroom materials: pencils, paper, markers, scissors, a blackboard or flip chart, and tape.

Note: In Part Two (sessions 8-16), the format of the group shifts as teens choose a change they want to focus on. Each week they will try out tools to manage their transitions. In these sessions, the core activities are group discussion and writing/ reflection. Because teens will be thinking deeply about situations in their own lives, the group can become emotional. For tips on how to manage these sessions, see the introduction to Part Two on p. 84 of this guide.

Do I Have to Do All of the Activities?

Try to complete all of the activities in each workshop. Most of the activities build on one another, so the workshop will lose something if you skip them.

Do I Have to Follow the Times?

The time suggested for each activity is a recommendation. The interest level of your group and issues that come up in discussion may cause you to go longer or shorter than the suggested time for an activity. But note that if your workshop has a fixed time and you go longer on one activity you'll have to cut back on another. Use your judgment.

Food, Rituals, and Ceremonies

Making this workshop feel like a special place by providing food, and incorporating rituals and ceremonies, can contribute greatly to the group spirit and process.

Workshop participants always welcome food. In most sessions you won't want to spend a lot of time eating, but you can have snacks on a side table, for example, that people can get up and eat as they please. Or you could schedule a 10-minute "working" snack break in the middle of each session. (You may want to ask the teens what would work best for them. If the workshop is after school and they arrive hungry, having food at the beginning may work best. If it's on a weekend morning, they may appreciate a snack break mid-workshop.)

There are many ways to build rituals and ceremonies into the workshops as well, which may or may not incorporate food. We encourage group leaders to pick a few that work for them.

For example, one of our groups asked to begin each session with tea and hot chocolate to set a cozy and relaxed tone. Some groups may want to start with a deep breathing exercise or guided meditation, or end with each person contributing a closing thought or reflection on the day.

Have some suggestions in mind and then talk with your group about what they would like. This can create a special bond.

Who Should Read?
A Note on How to Read the Stories

There are three ways to read the stories. Volunteers can take turns reading them aloud. You can read them aloud to the students. Or teens can read them silently (before or during the session).

The most active approach, and the one we recommend in most instances, is to have the teens read the stories aloud. It engages them and is good reading practice.

For particularly weak readers, consider assigning just a paragraph or a sentence. But try to give everyone a chance, and be encouraging and supportive. You may even want to talk with the group about how important it is

to become a strong reader. And explain that they can play an important role in supporting each other, especially the teens who are struggling.

If you are a very good reader or have dramatic training, you may want to read the stories to the teens yourself—at least from time to time. But doing so cuts down on the teens' participation. It can also be harder to stop and ask questions while you are reading aloud to teens, and asking questions is a good way to gauge comprehension and involve those who are hesitant to read aloud.

Helpful Words

Here are a few of the key concepts you'll be exploring in the Transitions program. Your teens will find a copy of this list on p. 4 of the Teen Journal. Use it as a reference whenever your students need more clarification.

Words About Transitions

Change: Change is what's different. One day you have a job, or a girlfriend, the next day you don't. That's a change. Often change is outside of your control, like being forced to switch homes or schools. But you can also choose change, like quitting a bad job. Change is a constant in life. This workshop will help you learn to manage it better.

Transition: How you react and adapt to the change *on the inside*. A change, like losing a girlfriend, can happen in one day, but the transition—grieving for your loss and being single again—can take much longer.

Tools (coping mechanisms): Things we do to manage difficult changes and transitions. For example, one coping mechanism when moving to a new home might be to spend a lot of time in your room until you feel more settled, or to talk out your anxieties with a supportive friend. In transitions, we call positive coping mechanisms "tools."

Words About Making a Good Group

Constructive feedback: Responding to people in a way that is helpful to them. The more we can learn to provide constructive feedback (instead of criticism or advice) the more successful this workshop will be.

Ground rules: The rules we set for how we get along in the group; these should be designed to promote a trusting and supportive atmosphere.

Advice: Telling someone what you would do or what you think they should do (in the workshop, we try to avoid this).

Support: Helping someone decide what they want to do; supporting their actions or emotions without judging.

Reflection: Thinking about what happened, your feelings, the choices you made, the good and bad consequences, and what you'll do differently the next time. Reflection gives you the power to respond differently the next time you confront a problem instead of getting trapped in the same cycle over and over again.

PART I
Learning About Transitions

SESSIONS 1-7

In the first seven sessions, teens will learn about change and transition and reflect on examples from their own lives. They will be introduced to the stages of transition (Letting Go, Chaos, and New Start) and will learn about the strategies (tools) they can use to manage the transitions process in their lives.

Session 1: Welcome! Introduction to Transitions

Workshop Summary

Teens become acquainted with each other and are introduced to the background of the Transitions program and its fundamental concepts.

Time: 2 hours* (see note)

Materials: Whiteboard/flipchart, markers, pen

Story: "A Method to the Madness" [p. 27]

Goals:
1. Teens will get to know each other and begin building trust.
2. Teens will be introduced to the Transitions concepts and background.
3. Teens will identify and share personal goals for the workshop.
4. Teens will identify meaningful transitions from their lives.

*Note: Consider kicking off the workshop with a welcome meal or snacks so that participants and leaders get to know each other in a relaxed social atmosphere. You may want to add half an hour to the beginning or the end of the first workshop for this.

Activity 1: Introduction (15 min)

This first workshop session should set the tone for the entire series by feeling relaxed and comfortable, yet structured. Enthusiastically welcome teens and provide a simple, brief introduction to the purpose of the workshop.

 Say something like this (in your own words):

Welcome to the Transitions workshop! We are all here to work on something very important: learning how to cope with and manage big changes in our lives.

Sometimes it can feel like we don't have a lot of control over the changes that happen to us. Can anyone here relate to that?

Well, every person on the planet feels that way at times of major change in their lives. But there are ways that we can manage our emotional response to big changes, and that's what we're here to explore together.

So what is this Transitions Framework? It's a program that was first developed for the corporate world, where people who work for big companies often go through changes (lay-offs, new assignments, etc.). Is getting laid off from your job a big change? How about changing jobs?

The Transitions Framework was designed for corporate people and later adapted for youth in foster care, who often go through even bigger and more intense changes. It's a way to learn about how change happens, be aware of how you're feeling during a change, and learn new ways to cope with a change.

Here are some important things for you to think about during the weeks we spend together:

* The things you'll learn in the course of the workshop about making successful transitions can be applied to situations throughout your life—because change keeps coming. We'll start learning some strategies now, and you'll get better and better at these strategies the more you use them.

* The Transitions Framework can be used by anyone—not just teens in care. You're going to be learning things that many adults haven't figured out yet, and that's going to give you a head start on managing future transitions, whether they're situations you experience in foster care, when you're aging out of care, or professional and personal situations in your adult lives.

* Change happens over and over again, to everybody, and it's often difficult. Learning better ways to deal with change will help you throughout your life.

To the Reader

This journal will change your life. (But only if you use it.)

Doing the activities in this journal will give you the power to control the transitions in your life, instead of being controlled by them. For example, most youth in foster care have had to move to new homes and live with new families, often multiple times. You have a right to be angry about those changes. But how you manage and express that anger can have a big impact on whether you get what you want out of life.

We do have to warn you, it won't be easy. Real change is always hard. But if you're willing to put in the time and effort, this journal—and the whole Transitions program—can help you learn how to manage changes and transitions in ways that lead you toward your goals.

How do we know that? Many teens in foster care participated in workshops to help develop these activities, and we refined the program each time based on their feedback. You can have confidence that we've created a program that will really work, if you give it your best.

In the first half of the workshop, we'll start getting to know each other, and learn about the Transitions process—how in every change you make, you generally go through several different stages of transition, and how there are "tools" that can help you get through and deal with the change you're facing.

Then, in the second half of the workshop, you'll have a chance to try out those tools, as you work on a change you want to make in your own life. Each week you'll come back to the group and talk about how it went: What worked? What didn't? What was fun? Challenging? Scary? Rewarding? With the help of your peers and the facilitator, you will grow and change. Most importantly, you will be honing skills that you can use in the next transition in your life, and the next,

and the next. You will be building the "Transitions process" into the emotional memory of your life.

In the final workshop, you will celebrate the progress you have made. And you will discover several things. First, you will have made real change. Second, you will have developed skills and insights that you can use again and again. Third, you will be very proud of yourself—and of everyone in the group. Finally, you will feel more confident that no matter what life throws at you, you'll have the ability to respond in ways that helps you achieve your goals, instead of setting you back.

Thanks for using this journal. We hope the program is as helpful to you as it was to us.

Sincerely,

The Transitions Teens

Miguel Ayala   Connie Harland
Yuhenna Burns   Cynthia Dubes
Samantha Flowers   Michael Dri
Armando Goodwin   Hattie Kim
Pauline Gordon   Henny Sanchez
Silva Harrigan   Natasha Santos
Gilbert Howard   Samantha Young

P.S. We've included several of our workshop journals at the end of this journal (and a couple of them are included with the activities). If you're curious, they will give you an idea of what we were thinking while we took the workshop, and what we worked on.

3

• Next, pass out the Teen Journals. Explain that teens will be completing many activities in these journals during the course of the workshop. When the workshop is over, they will be able to take the journals home, and will have a good record of the work they've done here.

• Ask teens to turn to the journal introduction (p. 3) and ask for volunteers to take turns reading aloud. The introduction provides a good overview of the workshop. Afterwards, answer any questions your group has about what to expect.

Activity 2: Find Someone Who....
(15 minutes)

Note: We recommend that you participate in this activity too. It will give the teens a chance to know you as a person and not just as the leader of the group.

 Say (in your own words):

Since we're going to be spending a lot of time together over the coming weeks and talking about some personal things, it's important that we start getting to know each other.

We're going to do an icebreaker where we find out things we have in common with other people in the room.

• Ask teens to turn to the "Find Someone Who…" bingo sheets in their journals (p. 11). Ask one of the teens to read aloud the instructions at the top of the sheet, then tell them to begin.

• Monitor the group interactions and give an encouraging nudge to any teens who seem hesitant to participate, as well as to any teens who are not mingling (i.e., sticking with one partner). Keep things positive. Let teens mingle for about

Session 1: Welcome! Introductions and Orientation to Transitions

Find Someone Who....

You have 10 minutes to ask other people in the group the questions on the bingo squares, with the goal of filling in as many squares as possible. Try to talk to as many people as you can. Introduce yourself to the other person, then ask them a question.

When you find someone who can respond "yes" to a question, *have them sign their name in the square on your bingo sheet* and then move on to the next person. For some questions, you also need to get a piece of info, such as what the person's sign is. Good luck!

Find someone who...

Expects to graduate from high school	Has an artistic talent Talent: _____	Gets excited about change	Has had a job Job: _____	Knows their astrological sign Sign: _____
Has lost a job	Has more than two siblings	Has a pet Kind of Pet: _____	Has broken up with a close friend	Is studying for a GED
Has broken up with a boyfriend or girlfriend	Doesn't like pizza	FREE	Sees the glass half full	Has attended more than five schools
Plans to go to college	Knows what career s/he wants Career goal: _____	Has gone through a big loss	Doesn't like change	Likes to dance
Has made a sacrifice to help someone else	Likes to stand out from the crowd	Is shy	Has a high school diploma	Likes to play video games Favorite: _____

11

10 minutes, then call the group back together to debrief.

 Debrief by asking:

> *Are you used to going up to people and introducing yourself? How did that feel?*

> *Did you have things in common with other people in the room? What kinds of things did you have in common? (Ask for examples.) How did that feel?*

Note: It will be fun, interesting, and reassuring for teens to find that they have things in common. Underscore those similarities to begin building the group.

Activity 3: Imagining a Transition
(25 minutes)

Note: Although this activity involves a long script, it's a simple and fun exercise in which teens will see that

Transitions is not just for "foster kids" or teenagers—it's a process that adults need help with as well. Read the script to yourself before you do the activity with teens; you can easily adapt it.

- Tell teens to open their journals to the "Corporate Character" worksheet (p. 12). In order to emphasize that the Transitions Framework is applicable to everyone—and at any stage in life—participants will imagine a corporate executive about to lose his/her job.

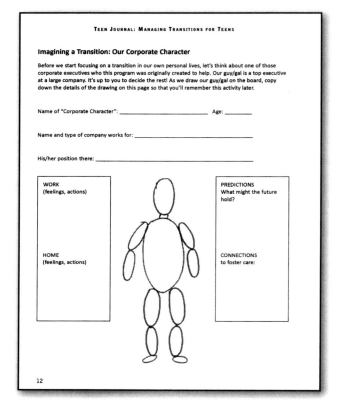

TEEN JOURNAL: MANAGING TRANSITIONS FOR TEENS

Imagining a Transition: Our Corporate Character

Before we start focusing on a transition in our own personal lives, let's think about one of those corporate executives who this program was originally created to help. Our guy/gal is a top executive at a large company. It's up to you to decide the rest! As we draw our guy/gal on the board, copy down the details of the drawing on this page so that you'll remember this activity later.

Name of "Corporate Character": _____ Age: _____

Name and type of company works for: _____

His/her position there: _____

WORK (feelings, actions)

HOME (feelings, actions)

PREDICTIONS What might the future hold?

CONNECTIONS to foster care:

12

- Ask a volunteer to read the introduction at the top of the page. Then ask for another volunteer to come to the board and copy the diagram: Draw the outline of a person, along with the headings "WORK," "HOME," "PREDICTIONS," and "CONNECTIONS TO FOSTER CARE," as shown on the worksheet.

 **Tell the teens:**

> *OK, now let's create our character:*

What kind of company does this character work for?

Is it a male or female?

What's our character's name?

How old?

What's the race/ethnicity?

Hairstyle?

Style of dress?

What very important position does s/he hold?

• Have the volunteer draw in the details as the group provides them. Remind the group to copy the drawing in the space provided on their worksheet (so that they will stay engaged and remember the point of this activity later on). This activity is a good way to lighten up the group: so long as the character remains somewhat realistic, participants will enjoy embellishing a bit.

 Tell the teens:

Now, _____has been a top executive at this Very Important Company for about 10 years, but in the last few years, the company's been struggling and it's just been bought out by an Even More Important Company and _____ will be losing his/ her job in just three months.

Every day s/he goes to work and knows that that very important position s/he has will soon be no more. S/he has no idea what comes next. So who can tell me what s/he might be feeling every day when s/he goes to work? Just give me some emotions.

• List responses under the heading "WORK." Teens will probably say things like: scared, angry, unmotivated, jealous, insecure, mistreated,

abandoned, feeling like life is unfair. If not, elicit these responses. Then, ask teens how these feelings might lead him/her to act at work. Add these responses under "WORK" (e.g., slacks off, is hostile to boss or co-workers, works overtime hoping to be kept on, etc.)

 Tell the teens:

OK, at the end of the day, _____ goes home. Who's at home?

• Have teens share responses aloud—spouse, children, dog, cat, grandma, etc.

 Tell the teens:

How does _____ behave at home now that s/he knows s/he's going to lose his/her job? How does s/he act out his/her feelings? Does s/he talk about it? Scream? Sit silently? Does s/he leave the family altogether? What does s/he feel when s/he is lying in bed at the end of the day?

• Invite responses and list them under the heading "HOME."

 Tell the teens:

So _____ is not in a very good place emotionally. S/he's feeling….(read responses from board). S/he's acting…. (read responses from board) because s/ he's losing the old identity and old sense of security and s/he has no idea what's coming next. S/he has to deal with a lot of stress, and s/he has to deal with a lot of uncertainty and chaos.

But of course that doesn't mean what will come next is going to be bad. It doesn't mean it's going to be good, either. But for the moment _____ has no idea what the outcome will be.

Just for the heck of it, who can imagine some possible outcomes for _____? Give me some good ones and some bad ones. Where will s/he be in a year or five years?

• List ideas that the teens come up with under heading "PREDICTIONS". Responses could include things like: Get another/better job: start his/her own company; take another job in the same field for less money; switch careers; never work again; lose house and family; get by working odd jobs but family remains strong; etc. Choose a couple of these predicted outcomes and ask the teens what might be good and bad about those outcomes.

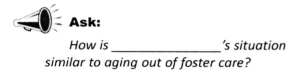 **Ask:**

How is _____'s situation similar to aging out of foster care?

• Write responses on the board under the "CONNECTIONS TO FOSTER CARE" heading. Ask participants to copy the responses onto the worksheet in the space provided.

 **Tell the teens:**

Let's return to _____ for a minute. When _____ first learns that s/he's losing the job, does s/he know what the future is going to be? No.

S/he may get another better job in a few weeks, but it may be months or even years before _____ has the same kind of confidence and certainty that s/he had when s/he was at that Very Important Company.

Or s/he may never find that kind of

stability again.

But s/he may learn some lessons along the way, like how s/he is able to adapt to all kinds of situations, and that s/he is more flexible and creative in putting together a satisfying life than s/he ever realized.

 Tell the teens:

What the Transitions workshop is all about is helping you, or _____, or anyone else responding to a major change to be able to deal with endings and loss and the chaos of not knowing what comes next.

Because that's what happens when you experience a major change, like aging out of foster care.

We hope the workshop also helps you figure out some new tools, or strategies, as well as show you some that you already use to cope with change, so that you can begin to take steps to create a new start.

 Tell the teens:

One of the most important lessons that we hope you'll learn during this workshop is that all the feelings that you might experience when a change hits you—the anger, fear, acting out, and total confusion, feelings of abandonment and that life isn't fair, worries about whether you'll make it—these are all normal and natural and to be expected.

And one of the points of the Transitions workshop is that you need to find active ways to experience and express those feelings. You need to give voice to them and allow them, because doing that is part of the process that will help you be ready to make a new start.

• Finally, invite participants to add to the worksheet any other thoughts they have. Remind them that it may be helpful to look over this worksheet later in the workshop to keep them focused on big picture goals.

Activity 4: Introducing the Stages of Transition (30 min)

 Tell the teens:

Every time we experience a change, we also have an emotional reaction to it that we have to manage (which is called a transition). And one of the main ideas behind the Transitions Framework is that a transition (the process of adapting and adjusting emotionally to a change) doesn't happen all at once—it happens in stages.

For example, one change that happens to a lot of people is going through a break-up. A break-up is a change that can take a long time to get used to. So it's a good way to look at the stages you go through in a transition.

Let's start at the beginning: Say your boyfriend or girlfriend broke up with you this morning. How are you feeling right now? How are you going to be feeling for the next couple days or weeks or months?

• Elicit some emotions from the group, and write them on the board in one column. Answers could include: sad, depressed, angry, in denial, grief-stricken, shocked, relieved.

 Ask:

How might you be behaving? How might you be dealing with all these things you're feeling?

This Morning

> *Feelings*
>
> | sad | shocked |
> | depressed | relieved |
> | angry | grief stricken |
> | in denial | |
>
> *Behavior*
>
> crying
> eating junk food
> listening to sad music
> talking to a friend

• Draw a line under the emotion words and list the behaviors, which might include: crying, eating junk food, listening to sad music, trying to argue with the person or convince them to take you back, talking to a friend, using drugs or alcohol.

 Say:

OK, so say a few months have passed now. You're no longer feeling so shocked or angry, but you're not feeling totally normal either. You're still trying to figure out who you are without this other person in your life. You're struggling with things like who to call when you just want to talk, or how to respond if someone flirts with you. How do you think you'd be feeling at this point?

• List responses on the board in a second column, next to the first. Elicit responses like: confused, lonely, excited (at the prospect of finding someone new, or at having time to yourself), depressed, still sad sometimes.

 **Ask:**

How do you think you might you be acting? What might you be doing to deal with how you're feeling?

• Draw a line under the emotion words and list responses, which might include things like: staying at home all the time, hooking up with lots of different people, trying new activities or joining new clubs, reconnecting with old friends, hanging out with a new crowd, throwing yourself into a new relationship.

 Say:

Finally, and this may be a few weeks or months later, or even longer than that, you get to the point where you hardly ever think about your ex, and if you do think about him or her, it doesn't make you upset. You may be in a new relationship that makes you happy, or you may have found a way to enjoy being single.

How are you feeling now?

• List responses on the board in a third column. Elicit words like: happy, calm, at peace, balanced, comfortable.

 Ask:

How are you acting?

• Draw a line under the emotion words and list actions like: going out with friends, dating, having fun.

 Tell the teens:

So there are roughly three different stages we went through here. In the Transitions Framework, we call this first stage Letting Go. (Label the top of the first column Letting Go.) That's when you're grieving over whatever you've lost in this change.

You have to let go of the way things were. It can be a very sad time.

Even if the change you're making is a good one (like if you're the one who chose to end the relationship) you still want to acknowledge what you're losing and take

A few months later

Feelings	
confused	depressed
lonely	still sad sometimes
excited	

Behavior
staying at home all the time
hooking up with lots of people
trying new activities
reconnecting with old friends

Even later

Feelings	
happy	balanced
calm	comfortable
at peace	

Behavior
going out with friends
dating
having fun

the time to think about what it meant to you.

The second stage is called "Chaos" (Label on chart.) That's when things are up in the air and chaotic. You've let go of what you used to have, but you haven't adjusted to a new way of doing things yet.

In this case, you still haven't gotten used to being without the other person. So you might feel confused or lost. But you might also feel hopeful or excited, since there are possibilities for something new and perhaps better than what you had before.

And this last stage we call "New Start." (Label on chart.) It's when you've finally really adjusted to the change and are comfortable with things being different.

Thinking about the thing or person you lost might always make you feel a little sad. But when you can talk about the change without reliving all the strong and painful emotions, you know you've made a new start.

 **Ask:**

What's the point of thinking about transitions this way? Why should we bother thinking about these three stages and labeling them? Does anyone have any thoughts on how this could help you adjust to a change better?

• Give students some time to respond. Elicit: The stages can help you remember that, even when a bad change happens, you're not always going to be stuck feeling sad and depressed about it—that you will eventually move through the other stages.

Thinking about the stages can help you realize where you are in terms of dealing with a change. It can be reassuring to know that if you just can't

stop feeling sad or angry about a change, it's because you're still in the process of letting go. Even if other people are telling you to move on and get over it, the Transitions Framework shows that you need to express and work through those feelings first, before you will be able to move on.

• Finally, draw students' attention to the behaviors at the bottom of each column. Point out that these are all strategies people use to deal with the feelings they're having. Point out that some strategies are healthy and positive (like talking to a friend) while others can be unhealthy or dangerous (like using drugs or being promiscuous).

Explain that the Transitions Framework includes positive strategies—called "tools"—that you can use to deal with the feelings of each stage in a healthy way, and that can help get you through. Note that we'll be learning about these tools in a few weeks, and then we'll try them out on changes in our own lives.

Activity 5: Story: "A Method to the Madness" (30 minutes)

• Ask teens to turn to Natasha's introduction to the Transitions workshop, "A Method to the Madness," on p. 13 in their journals. (You'll find a copy of the story on the next page of this guide.) Explain that this story was written by a teen in the very first Transitions group: it will help teens learn how to put the Transitions concepts into action, and how the group can support each other through that process.

• Take turns reading the story out loud. Encourage teens to underline or star important ideas that they connect with, agree or disagree with, or have questions about.

• Pause from time to time during the reading to ask teens the questions suggested in the margins of this guide, or any others you think might be helpful to your group.

Closing Reflection (5 minutes)

Direct teens to the Closing Reflection section of their journals. Give teens 5 or 10 minutes to write their responses in their journals. If you have time, you may ask for volunteers to share some of what they wrote.

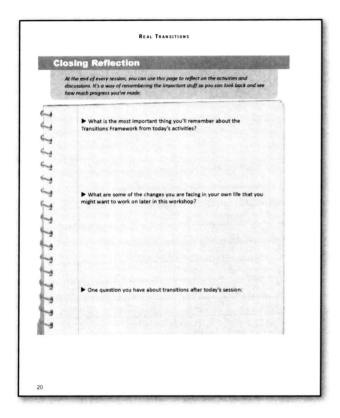

REAL TRANSITIONS

Closing Reflection

At the end of every session, you can use this page to reflect on the activities and discussions. It's a way of remembering the important stuff so you can look back and see how much progress you've made.

▶ What is the most important thing you'll remember about the Transitions Framework from today's activities?

▶ What are some of the changes you are facing in your own life that you might want to work on later in this workshop?

▶ One question you have about transitions after today's session:

20

A Method to the Madness
Learning new tools can
make changes easier to handle

Natasha Santos

By Natasha Santos

Last year I made a typical change: switching from one school to another because I wasn't doing well. For me, this change symbolized rejection and failure.

Leaving my school brought up too many old feelings that I wasn't ready to deal with, so I didn't. I spent half my school days in my bedroom, asleep or watching television. When I did go to school I mostly roamed the halls. Some days, I went to class and felt determined to change. But I didn't. It was a lot harder to manage the transition than I'd thought.

Overwhelming Changes

By the time teens are ready to leave care, we've dealt with lots of practical changes, like changing schools and homes several times. So you would think we'd get good at managing transitions, and that when it's time for the big change (aging out) we'd be prepared because we've

Q. We've all heard the expression "Practice makes perfect." So why might someone who's had a lot of experience going through changes in their life still not be good at handling change?

Q. What's the difference between making a change and managing a transition? (Have teens try to state the concepts in their own words, but don't worry about getting it exactly right—this isn't school.)

done it so often. But being forced to change doesn't make us good at it.

Changes bring up difficult emotions and memories that we haven't dealt with, and many times we get overwhelmed or depressed. Luckily, in the Transitions workshop we learned that there are ways to handle changes that we can practice so we can manage transitions more successfully in the future. These *tools* can be helpful and even fun.

New Ways to Handle Change

The first thing we had to understand was the difference between change and transition. Basically, a *change* is an event that happens, like changing schools, losing a loved one, making a friend, etc. Sometimes we choose to make the change, sometimes we don't.

A *transition* is what we go through emotionally, on the inside, to make sense of and adapt to that change. Both positive and negative changes require us to manage emotions.

Using the tools didn't change our past, or the emotions we were going through. But the tools did help us understand what we were feeling and gave us helpful ways to keep moving forward in our lives.

For the workshop, each of us chose a change we *wanted* to make (for example, finding more supportive friends, or being less self-critical). But you can also use the tools to deal with a change that just happens to you, like changing foster homes or schools. Each week we talked about how our changes were going, and wrote a diary about how we handled our transitions.

The Three Stages of Transitions

Next, we learned about the three major stages of a transition:

Letting Go: You first must realize that a change is taking place, and say goodbye to the old way. Recognizing what you will be losing and accepting it is the hardest part, because that often brings up other losses.

Chaos: During this time, you've let go of your old way but haven't yet found a new way, so you have a lot of confusion and fear. It's uncomfortable, but it can also be a time of discovery.

New Start: You begin to feel comfortable and have accepted the change. You're excited by the new goals that you're working toward.

Getting From One Stage to Another

There are coping strategies (we called them "tools") you can use in each of the stages to make your transitions smoother. For example, in the Chaos stage you might use a reflection tool, like writing in a journal, when you are feeling confused. Or to celebrate the progress you've made in reaching New Start, you could reward yourself with little things like a chocolate shake or even a certificate you make for yourself.

Everyone naturally uses some of these tools. When my friend Pauline moved into a new foster home, she used this tool to manage the chaos: "Surround yourself with things that remind you of good times or make you feel comfortable, peaceful, at home."

Pauline wrote: "Living in a stranger's home has been a difficult change. My room is where I recuperate, where

Q. Think about a big change you went through in the past. Did you have trouble Letting Go? Were you uncomfortable or freaked out during Chaos? Did you reach New Start? (Ask the teens to share some examples.)

I can gather my thoughts and feel at home. I've framed pictures or have items lying around that remind me of all the people and things that make me happy. My plant I've grown since I was living at my grandmother's house reminds me of warm memories shared back home…"

The point of the workshop, though, was to get us to experiment with tools that don't come naturally, and take a risk to try one out every week to really work on our change.

Q. What kind of "tools" or coping strategies come naturally to you? What are the things you usually do when you are dealing with a stressful situation?

Trying Out New Methods

For the first part of the workshop we thought about changes from our past that were still affecting us, and then learned new tools for managing our emotional responses to those changes.

Then we picked one change we were struggling with *right now*. We mapped out a 10-week plan of what we wanted to achieve, and the tools we would use each week.

Erica wanted to begin to remember and create good memories. She could only remember bad things from her childhood and often dwelled on those bad feelings. Michael's goal was to figure out which friends he could trust and which he didn't feel comfortable around.

Hattie criticized herself harshly and constantly. She wanted to work on changing the negative script in her head. Pauline worked on preparing herself for independence from foster care despite having little support.

I chose to work on my transition from my old school to my new school, to go from cutting classes to attending them. I wanted to figure out ways to develop relationships with people in the school and also feel more a part of school in general.

Could We Let Go of Old Ways?

We were all excited, but we were worried, too. Could we change? Were we capable of letting go of the old ways that were holding us back? The idea of making a change seems good, but the actual work and that goes into that is scary and uncomfortable. I guess that's why so many people stay stuck in their ways.

We were also uneasy about letting go of our old defenses, and having to re-think some things that life had taught us. Like Hattie: Her parents taught her to look on the dark side of life and to believe that life will always be painful and difficult. By choosing to change and going through the process of transition, Hattie would be saying that the way she had been raised was not OK with her anymore. In a way, she'd be saying goodbye to a belief in her parents and to ideas that had been stuck in her brain since childhood.

Getting Support from the Group

To keep us on track, we met weekly to discuss the tools we used and to give each other feedback on our progress.

Trust in the group didn't come naturally. All of us felt uneasy about exposing so much of ourselves. Michael dealt with this by keeping his distance. While the group sat in a circle, Michael sat about a foot outside it.

But sometimes we really were able to help each other. When Pauline wouldn't admit to wanting to make any changes in her life, we asked tons of questions and then sat and waited until she was ready to open up to us. She

Q. Think about a change that you made or wanted to make in your life that was difficult. What made it hard?

eventually did.

And when Hattie was negative about herself, we'd catch her and tell her not to put herself down. After a while, no more negative words came out of her mouth.

Q. How important is trust within a group like ours? Why do you feel that way?

Noticeably Changed

Everybody had made progress by the end of the group. Michael began to recognize that his concerns about his friends came from not letting them know what he's comfortable with.

Erica discovered happier childhood memories through conversations with her mother, and took pictures for her scrapbook that reminded her of good times.

Pauline kept herself motivated at handling her job and college plans, and applied for financial support and housing so she could more easily leave care. And Hattie stopped beating herself up.

As for me, I was going to class and enjoying in my new school.

By the end, I think we all felt a little more confident so that when we need to handle huge changes like aging out, starting college, or beginning a new job, we'll have the ability to manage those transitions.

More Ready for Independence

Usually when we think about growing up, we think about practical changes like finishing school and finding housing and a job. But the more difficult changes might be the emotional transitions we need to make inside: From negatives to positives, from bad relationships to stronger ones, and to independence, communication and remembering the good times.

Emotional independence—the ability to deal with our emotions and our problems—is what will give us the ability to handle those practical changes, and it's the one thing no one can give us. We have to learn on our own, by making mistakes, trying new ways of handling feelings we've had for years. Learning the tools, and using them, is a start.

Q. Do you think you can learn emotional independence without making mistakes? Why or why not?

Session 2: Building a Safe and Supportive Group

Workshop Summary

Teens continue to build trust, support, and communication as they establish group norms and expectations and learn how to share constructive feedback.

Time: 2 hours

Materials: Whiteboard/flip chart, markers, pens, sticky notes

Story: "Digging Deep in My Soul" [p. 39]

Goals:

1. The group will develop rules and guidelines for the workshops that everyone can agree on.
2. The teens will understand the role of constructive feedback, setting personal boundaries, and confidentiality in creating a positive and productive group dynamic.
3. The teens will understand the difference between giving someone advice and providing support, and why providing support is preferred for this program.

Activity 1: Counting Game (10 min)

 Tell the teens:

Today we'll work together to figure out ways that we can support each other and feel supported as we go through the workshop.

You all are going to spend most of this session coming up with expectations and guidelines our group should follow in order to make a comfortable, supportive atmosphere for everyone. But right now, we're going to play a very simple game.

• Direct teens to the first page of the "Counting Game" activity in their journals and read the instructions.

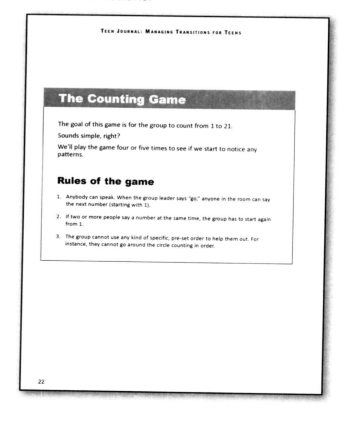

TEEN JOURNAL: MANAGING TRANSITIONS FOR TEENS

The Counting Game

The goal of this game is for the group to count from 1 to 21.

Sounds simple, right?

We'll play the game four or five times to see if we start to notice any patterns.

Rules of the game

1. Anybody can speak. When the group leader says "go," anyone in the room can say the next number (starting with 1).

2. If two or more people say a number at the same time, the group has to start again from 1.

3. The group cannot use any kind of specific, pre-set order to help them out. For instance, they cannot go around the circle counting in order.

22

Emotional independence—the ability to deal with our emotions and our problems—is what will give us the ability to handle those practical changes, and it's the one thing no one can give us. We have to learn on our own, by making mistakes, trying new ways of handling feelings we've had for years. Learning the tools, and using them, is a start.

Q. Do you think you can learn emotional independence without making mistakes? Why or why not?

Session 2: Building a Safe and Supportive Group

Workshop Summary

Teens continue to build trust, support, and communication as they establish group norms and expectations and learn how to share constructive feedback.

Time: 2 hours

Materials: Whiteboard/flip chart, markers, pens, sticky notes

Story: "Digging Deep in My Soul" [p. 39]

Goals:

1. The group will develop rules and guidelines for the workshops that everyone can agree on.
2. The teens will understand the role of constructive feedback, setting personal boundaries, and confidentiality in creating a positive and productive group dynamic.
3. The teens will understand the difference between giving someone advice and providing support, and why providing support is preferred for this program.

Activity 1: Counting Game (10 min)

 Tell the teens:

Today we'll work together to figure out ways that we can support each other and feel supported as we go through the workshop.

You all are going to spend most of this session coming up with expectations and guidelines our group should follow in order to make a comfortable, supportive atmosphere for everyone. But right now, we're going to play a very simple game.

• Direct teens to the first page of the "Counting Game" activity in their journals and read the instructions.

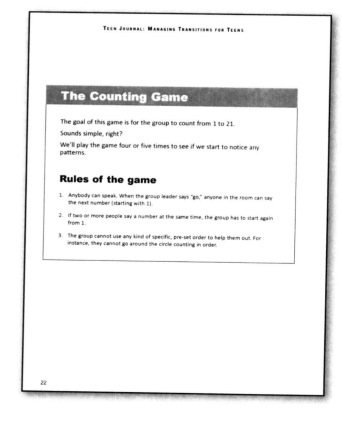

• Let the group try the game four or five times and see how they do. Then ask the group if they have any reactions. Who was taking charge? Who felt nervous to say a number at all? What helped the group become more successful (e.g., slowing down, eye contact)? What can we learn from this activity about how to work as a group?

Tell the teens:

This game is a way of noticing how the group is working together, who's taking what roles, who's charging ahead, who's holding back, how well people are paying attention to other people in the group, and whether the group is really working together to reach a common goal. `

Learning to work well in a group is important in this workshop, but it's also a very valuable skill in the rest of your life. So it's something we'll continue working on throught the workshop.

Activity 2: Setting Group Norms and Expectations
(55 minutes total for this activity)

Deciding on Goals (25 minutes)

Tell the teens:

Our job today is to think about our goals and come up with guidelines that all group members can agree on and respect in order to achieve what we want out of the workshop.

Working through transition can bring up some intense feelings, and you may want to share those feelings in the group. So it's important for us to establish trust and support for one another, and to have guidelines that help everyone feel comfortable.

• Pass out sticky notes, directing teens to take a few notes each.

Tell the teens:

Before we come up with our guidelines, we'd like you to think about goals—both your own goals for the workshop (what you want to accomplish here) and your goals for the group (what you think the group should be like).

For example, one of your goals might be to get a better perspective on a change that's happening in your life that you've been having a hard time with. Or it might be to speak up in the group, or to make sure you come on time.

Goals for the group might include things like creating a space where everyone feels comfortable, or having a group that's supportive.

• Ask teens to write one goal on each note (up to six). Remind them that they should include some individual goals, and some goals for the group. Tell them that these goals will be anonymous—they don't need to write their names.

• After everyone is done, collect all the sticky notes and post them on the board, with individual goals on one side and group goals on the other. Then, read them aloud with the group. Comment on any general themes you notice (e.g., "A lot of people want to tackle some big changes in their life," or, "A lot of people want the group to be safe, supportive and respectful.")

Creating the Guidelines (25 minutes)

Tell the teens:

So now that we know what we all want to get out of the workshop, and what we want our group to look like, we can set some ground rules that will help make sure we're able to accomplish these things.

These will be rules that we all agree to follow in the group. For instance, a lot of groups have a "one mic" rule—that means only one person should speak at a time, so if someone else is speaking you don't interrupt them.

• Pass out blank sheets of paper and ask teens to write down 3-5 ground rules that they'd like to have in the group.

• After a few minutes, ask for volunteers to share their rules, and write them on the board or a new piece of chart paper. Try to elicit a list that covers what the rules for participation/attendance will be, and how teens will behave toward each other in the group. If teens don't suggest all of these things, prompt them with questions like: How should people in the group respond when someone is sharing something personal? What would you not want other people in the group to do if you were sharing something? Should we have a rule about coming here on time? Etc.

As part of the discussion on respect, make sure to include a clear rule on cell phone use (e.g., cell phones must be turned off for the entire workshop; you can provide a contact number at your agency for emergencies.)

• Ultimately, it's important to elicit some variation of the following:

—Be on time.

—Attend every session. If you can't make it, you should call in advance, and try to catch up by talking with a teen who was in the workshop and doing as many of the worksheets as you can.

—Make an effort to fully and honestly participate in the group and do all of the activities.

—Listen to what others have to say, even though it may be painful at times.

—Respond to others with respect. When someone is talking, don't interrupt. Don't laugh, roll your eyes, turn away, start texting or otherwise not paying attention.

—Try to avoid giving advice and criticizing (e.g., saying things like "You should have done X."). Instead, listen and support (e.g., "That sounds really hard," or "When I was in a similar situation, I felt....and what helped me was...").

—Accept support and feedback from the group with respect. Listen to and consider what others offer, even if you ultimately decide you disagree.

—Don't gossip about people in the group.

—Don't tell others what we share. What's discussed in the room stays in the room.

Note: Make sure teens understand what "body language" means, and how you can show disrespect to someone else without saying anything bad or talking at all (e.g., by turning away, playing with your hair or your phone or other device, tapping your fingers or your foot impatiently, sighing, putting your head down on the table, rolling your eyes, grimacing, etc. while someone else is talking.)

Finally, ask whether anyone has any additions. It is important to give multiple opportunities to the teens to process and reflect so that they feel incorporated into the decision-making process.

Note: Leave this chart up during the session. Afterward, write up the guidelines on chart paper in an organized way and post it for reference in future sessions. This is very helpful for getting the group involved being supportive and monitoring each other's behavior and level of participation.

Activity 3: Advice versus Support
(30 minutes)

 Tell the teens:

One of the most important things in reaching the group goals we've set is our ability to tell the difference between giving advice and providing support. What do you think is the difference? Why might it be important to respond to each other with support rather than advice?

Clarify that advice means telling the other person what to do. When you offer someone support, you are helping them to think about their own situation and all their options, rather than making a decision for them.

• Direct teens to turn to the worksheet, "Giving Constructive Feedback: Advice vs. Support" (p. 23). Read it and the chart that fol-

lows aloud together.

• Then, ask students to look at the worksheet, "Advice vs. Support: Which is Which?" Read the instructions and give the students a few minutes to indicate which statements are supportive and which are advice. (You'll find an answer key on the next page of this guide.)

When they're done, ask them why some questions feel supportive and others feel like advice. Which kind of feedback do they prefer?

• Now, direct everyone to turn to the story, "Digging Deep in My Soul" (p. 27 in the Teen Journal, p. 39 in this guide).

Tell students that this is a true story a young man wrote about dealing with loss. Ask for volunteers to read a few paragraphs each.

Giving Constructive Feedback
Advice vs. Support

Adults frequently give teens advice, rather than support, and teens often hate it. Yet, if you listen closely, teens can also fall into the habit of giving advice to their friends, when what a friend really needs is support!

What's the difference between advice and support? When a friend is going through a hard time, it's natural to want to help and give advice. But when you give *advice*, you are telling the other person what to do instead of helping them to see all the options and make the best decision for them. (By jumping in and telling them what you would do, you've made a judgment about the best course of action.)

When you offer someone *support*, you are inviting them to think about their own situation, instead of trying to make decisions for them. That keeps them in charge of their own decisions, which is important in learning how to feel independent and in charge of our own lives instead of feeling helpless and unsure.

The difference between advice and support is in the way that you approach a person. Support means doing things like asking them questions to help them clarify their thoughts and feelings. It can mean showing empathy without judgment—letting them know you can relate and "feel their pain." That feels very different from telling someone what to do.

Look at the chart on the next page. "Advice" is described on the left. "Support" is described on the right. Below those descriptions are examples of the kinds of language we use when giving advice and support. Think about how different it feels to hear advice statements than to receive statements of support.

23

Advice	Support
Giving advice usually means telling the person what to do, instead of offering them choices. That doesn't help someone think about what's the best choice for him/her. It can also make him/her feel like you doubt their ability to make good decisions. That doesn't help someone feel independent or confident.	Supportive statements let someone know that you are concerned about them, but that you respect their ability to make their own decisions. It can build someone's confidence and trust to let them know you understand where they're coming from without trying to force them to think the same way you do about a problem.
Advice can sound like judging and criticizing:	Support should sound more like suggesting, understanding, respecting:
You should just _____.	It sounds like _____ (what I hear you saying is _____).
Why don't you just _____.	I've read _____.
You're wrong. Do _____ instead.	I've heard _____.
That's not going to help you.	I feel upset when you say that because _____.
What you really need to do is _____.	What you're saying makes sense to me because _____.
	One thing that helped me was _____.

24

Advice/Support Answer Key

"Of course you're flipping...you keep going off your meds!"
☑ ADVICE ☐ SUPPORT

"Sometimes my meds make me feel worse that not taking them at all. One thing I've found helpful is speaking up and telling the psychiatrist what's happening so she can adjust the levels and try different drugs."
☐ ADVICE ☑ SUPPORT

"I think it's stupid to stay in a foster home where they don't treat you right."
☑ ADVICE ☐ SUPPORT

"It must be so hard to come home to a place where you don't feel welcome. I'm really sorry you're not getting any support from your foster mom."
☐ ADVICE ☑ SUPPORT

"Of course you're broke—you spend all your money on hair, clothes, and eating out."
☑ ADVICE ☐ SUPPORT

"I used to be broke. I know from my own experience that it can be hard to save money when you're not used to it. Does anyone have any good strategies?"
☐ ADVICE ☑ SUPPORT

"I've found that when I'm really anxious or angry if I take 10 really deep breaths the feelings get a lot less intense."
☐ ADVICE ☑ SUPPORT

"You've got an anger problem. You just need to deal with it."
☑ ADVICE ☐ SUPPORT

Advice or Support: Which Is Which?

Read the follow statements. Indicate which statements are advice and which are support.

_____

"I think you should break up with him."
☑ ADVICE ☐ SUPPORT

"I also went with a guy who was verbally abusive. It made me feel really bad about myself. Is there anything we can do to help you?"
☐ ADVICE ☑ SUPPORT

"You should reach out to your father."
☑ ADVICE ☐ SUPPORT

"What do you think will happen if you reach out to your father? What do you want to have happen? Have you tried to reach out to him in the past?"
☐ ADVICE ☑ SUPPORT

"When I reached out to my dad it was hard at first, but we made sure to talk with each other each week and we grew closer."
☐ ADVICE ☑ SUPPORT

"I think I understand your frustration. Whenever I talk with my dad it feels like he's not really listening."
☐ ADVICE ☑ SUPPORT

"If you would just go to therapy you'd feel a lot better."
☑ ADVICE ☐ SUPPORT

"I think therapy can be helpful, but it's also really scary to be honest with someone like that. It took me a long time to decide to go."
☐ ADVICE ☑ SUPPORT

Griffin Kinard is having a lot of trouble coping with some big losses in his life. He needs support.

Digging Deep in My Soul
It's been hard to deal with the deaths in my life

Griffin Kinard

By Griffin Kinard

My family was two million miles short of perfect. My father hit and abused my siblings and me for no reason. My mother left as soon as she could.

Then, social services came and separated me from my siblings. The pain that I felt from watching first my mother, then my father, then my brothers leave me was unforgettable. I felt betrayed by my own people. It just killed me to see my family torn away one by one.

After a few foster homes and a hospital I was placed at a residential treatment center, where I stayed for the next nine years. It was pure hell.

I thought the abuse and the separations were enough mental testing for one person. Then the people close to me started leaving me for good.

Rushing My Own Death

When I was 9, my father went from being a man of strength to a man who needed to be pushed around in a wheelchair. He died of AIDS.

After my father died, I became reckless. I acted like nothing mattered. Looking back, I see now that I was rushing my own death. I could not bear the thought of being alive.

I started to go off on my own all the time. I was so sad that I was nobody's friend, and that my family did nothing but mess with me.

Eventually, I thought that killing myself was the answer. I tried to kill myself over and over again, but I failed each and every time. I think that part of me wanted to live.

I wasn't crazy. I was just too small to have experienced all that abuse, my mother disappearing and my father dying.

A Good Knight Sleeps

It took me years of spazzing out to move on. Finally, I did. I calmed down a lot. But the fight wasn't over yet.

When I was 16, I was in class when my social worker came and got me and took me to her office. She told me, "Griffin, your brother was shot." I was not shocked to hear the news because my brother had been shot before.

So I replied, "OK, is he in the hospital? Can I see him?"

"No, Griffin. Your brother was shot and killed."

The feelings that came over me I cannot explain.

My social worker asked me if I was all right.

"Yeah, I'm fine," I told her. Then I walked out of her office, only to see a door with a glass window. I punched the glass, but was still not fine. I could not get what she said out of my head. I could not grasp the truth. I repeated to myself, "My brother is not dead."

Pure Sadness and Anger

I arrived outside with tears in my eyes and blood dripping from my right hand. I started walking toward the busy street (not knowing why) but a voice in my head stopped me. It reminded me that people looked up to me.

That made me stop and think about a few things. Like, why is it that I cause harm to myself every time something devastating happens to me?

The last time I saw my brother he was cold like an iceberg. I was convinced my brother no longer had a soul. I felt nothing but pure sadness and anger. I did not see the point of living anymore.

That night after burying my brother, I thought to myself, "I am a knight and so was my brother. A knight is someone who plays the game down to the last dollar. He doesn't give up. Once he's in, he's in."

People always told me that I was a bright kid and that I could go far. I didn't believe their words at the time. But remembering my brother in his coffin, I really understood that life was short and I needed to make the most of mine.

Another Loss

Soon I was moved to a group home, where too many things happened. But the good part was I got a mentor who came to see me damn near every weekend.

We were real cool. He was white, I was black. It looked like opposites do attract. We went to the movies every weekend. Holidays we spent at his place. It was awesome and I was really enjoying it, but like all good things, it came to an end.

It was two weeks before Thanksgiving that I last saw Dale. A week later I walked into the group home and sat down to watch some television when the supervisor called me down to his office. He told me that my mentor had passed.

I didn't know what to do or say. I just cried tears of confusion. I thought, "Just a week ago we were making plans for Thanksgiving, and his family is making plans to bury him now?"

The Light in Death

It is very hard to find light when life gives you nothing but chaos and devastating situations. Losing my mentor and my family, I wanted to break down, give up. I had feelings I could no longer explain. I did not express my feelings to anybody. They were too raw.

To get through it I had to dig deep into my soul. When I got some time alone I was able to sit back and look at my life. I wrote a poem about someone dying and speaking their last words to their loved one, telling them that they love them no matter what.

Finding out that I could put my emotions on paper made me feel tough and ready for what the world threw at me. Soon I learned how to channel my feelings into poetry to the point that now the pen and the pad are my two best friends.

'Embrace Your Future'

Today, I write a poem for damn near every situation I

go through. Writing all that sadness and painful madness down has made those feelings just part of my past.

Now I remind myself, "Death is just death, not something to tear you apart. It's what we all wish for—peace and quiet." My time will come, but for now I try to enjoy everything life throws at me and to stay focused on the long run.

I tell myself, "Keep your mother-loving head up. Be proud of your past, accept your present, and embrace your future." I can keep the ones I lost in mind, but I must move on with my life.

Activity 4: Simulation with Advice vs. Support (20 minutes)

 Tell the teens:

We've been talking about the difference between advice and support. While advice is not always a bad thing, we want to focus more on ways of communicating support to each other by listening carefully and offering non-judgmental responses when someone shares their feelings. That takes practice!

So we're going to try out our new techniques on Griffin, whose story we've just read. We don't have the real Griffin with us, but use your imagination.

As you saw, Griffin has experienced many serious losses in his life. Remember the three stages of transition we talked about last week? What stage is Griffin in? [Letting Go, since he's still trying to deal with the loss of all these loved ones and figure out his feelings. Or Chaos, since he's starting to get a handle on his feelings through writing.]

 Ask:

What are some of his losses?

What are some of the emotions that he expresses in his story?

Can anyone else relate to feeling that way? (Briefly allow for responses.)

 Tell the teens:

Our job is to show support for Griffin, using the kinds of "support prompts" that we've been practicing.

We want to avoid judging Griffin or telling him what to do. This will help us

become better able to support each other when it's our turn to open up.

 Tell the teens:

OK, so let's assume it's about one month since his mentor Dale died, and Griffin is still in the first stage of transition—the "Letting Go" stage.

That means he's dealing with a lot of confusion, anger, sadness and depression. He's clinging to memories of the people he's lost, but he wants to move forward.

Our goal is to help him feel safe enough in the group that he can communicate, as a first step in letting go.

• Now, **conduct the simulation**. You (the group leader) are going to play Griffin, and the teens will be the other members of the group.

You will share that you've lost a lot of people in your life and are feeling hopeless. You also say that you're not sure you're ready to go too deep into your past with the group. That's all you share with the group.

Tips for leader on "being" Griffin: This works best if you play Griffin as despondent and difficult to reach. Use body language that communicates this: crossed arms, head down, no eye contact, mumbling, limited gestures. Like some members of your group, Griffin would be hesitant about opening up and sharing the very difficult feelings and memories described in his story.

The group will likely be somewhat frustrated by his lack of interaction and feel challenged to "make" Griffin open up. This is likely to lead them to give Griffin lots of advice, even when specifically instructed not to. It's important that you, as Griffin, respond accordingly—if someone makes a supportive statement, reward that by having Griffin respond by opening up a bit more, making eye contact, raising his head, etc. If someone makes a classic advice statement, make sure body language and responses reflect that by closing down and making responses limited (mumbling, saying "I don't know," shaking your head, saying, "You guys don't know how it feels.")

If you notice that the group is giving lots of advice and not offering up supportive statements/questions, take a break from the simulation to do a brief check-in. Ask "How does Griffin seem to be reacting? How do you feel about that? Are we making more support statements or advice statements? Let's try to stick to support and see if Griffin responds differently."

Point out that Griffin will not feel supported unless the group members are able to share from their own experiences, communicate that they can identify with him in some way, and show him empathy. When you call them on this after the activity, it will provide an excellent opportunity to reinforce the difference between advice and support.

• After completing the simulation, discuss as a group the following questions:

 Ask:

What can we see in Griffin that he doesn't seem to see about himself?

What effect did using the "support" prompts have on Griffin, and on the group? What worked? What didn't work? How do you think things might have been different if we had used more "advice" prompts?

Did anyone have a strong desire to use the "advice" prompts? When? How did that feel? What did you do?

Closing Reflection (5 minutes)

Direct teens to the Closing Reflection section of their journals.

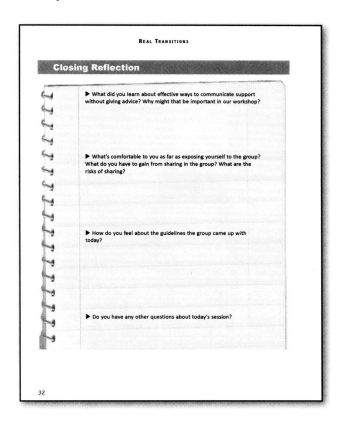

Session 3: Introducing the Tools

Workshop Summary

Teens identify "tools" they already use to cope with and manage transitions, and are exposed to new strategies, which they'll use to create a personalized toolbox in the following session.

Time: 2 hours

Materials: Bag of M&Ms, flipchart/whiteboard, blank paper, markers, pens, sticky notes

Goals:

1. Teens will learn that managing emotional transitions requires the use of tools, or strategies, to help us cope and adapt.
2. Teens will identify tools they already use to manage transitions, and be able to categorize them according to the Transitions Framework.
3. Teens will identify new tools that will be helpful to them.
4. Teens will create a "toolbox" of resources and strategies for managing transitions.

Activity 1: M&Ms Check-In (10 minutes)

• Invite each teen to take up to four M&Ms, telling them that for each M&M they take, they have to share one thing about themselves. One M&M is reserved for telling something—good or bad—that happened to them during the week, and one should be for sharing how they're feeling right now. The rest can be used to share any other things they want the group to know about them.

Note: Explain to teens that they'll use this activity to check in at the beginning of every session. This can be a time for them to mention anything that's on their mind, but make sure to note that the group won't have time to discuss anyone's situation in detail or give feedback.

The purpose of the check-in is not to get into an involved discussion of anyone's particular issues, nor is it to allow teens to excuse themselves from participating in the workshop that day. It's simply a space for everyone to decompress and let go of whatever is on their mind before they start the workshop.

Activity 2: Risks and Benefits of Looking Back (15 minutes)

 Tell the teens:

Today we're going to reflect on changes that we have experienced in the past. We'll look at things we did that were helpful, and other things that were not so helpful. Knowing how we've tended to react to change in the past will help us figure out the most helpful ways of facing change in the future.

This can be a difficult exercise, because it might remind us of painful experiences we've gone through. It can also be an exercise that makes us stronger, since if we are able to reflect on the past now, we will probably be more able to face those feelings when they resurface in the future, when we are trying to manage new transitions in our lives.

• Draw a two-column chart on the board with these headings:

Benefits	Risks

Tell the teens there are benefits and risks of reflecting on the past, and those are important to keep in mind. Ask them to write down on a blank sheet of paper three *benefits* of reflecting on the past, and three *risks*.

After a couple of minutes, go around the group and have teens read out what they have written down. Write their responses on the board and discuss.

Activity 3: Change vs. Transition
(30 minutes)

• Read aloud the "Change vs. Transition" worksheet on p. 34 in the Teen Journal. Give the group a couple of examples from your own life as a model.

• Ask teens to complete the chart on p. 35 in their journals. Circulate to check for understanding and verify that teens are differentiating between change and transition.

After about 15 minutes, ask for a few volunteers to share a change/transition they wrote about, or anything they noticed (e.g., do they

tend to react to change in the same ways every time, or have their responses changed as they've gotten older? Do they generally rely on the same kinds of strategies, or try different things? Etc.)

REAL TRANSITIONS

Change vs. Transition

In the Transitions workshop, we talk about change as something that happens outside of yourself, that you usually can't control. Change prompts a transition *inside of us* as we try to cope and adapt to new circumstances.

In the left-hand column, copy down several changes you've been through in your life. Then, in the right-hand column, describe the emotional transition you went through as you moved through that change. The first one is an example.

Changes in My Life — Things that happened (outside of you) When happened?	My Process of Transition — How you reacted and adapted to the change. What kinds of emotions did you go through as part of your transition? How did you cope?
CHANGE: Moved to a new school in fifth grade	TRANSITION: Felt angry, nervous and scared. I was fighting a lot. Then I got sent to the school social worker, who was nice. It made me feel relieved to have someone to talk to. I also made a few new friends. I started to feel calmer and safe.
CHANGE:	TRANSITION:
CHANGE:	TRANSITION:
CHANGE:	TRANSITION:

35

Activity 4: Recognizing Our Strengths
(25 minutes)

Ask participants to turn to p. 36 in their journals, an excerpt from Hattie Rice's diary "Flipping the Script." Ask for volunteers to take turns reading the story.

 Tell the teens:

Remembering to notice our strengths can really help when we're going through difficult experiences. We're now going to read a journal entry by Hattie Rice, who tried to do exactly that as a way of helping herself cope with hard times.

We were introduced to Hattie in the first workshop, when we read that she felt very negative about herself, and her goal was to see if she could find anything positive to hold onto.

Let's read this excerpt about Hattie discovering positive aspects of herself.

Remembering to notice our strengths can really help when we're going through difficult experiences. Hattie tried to do exactly that as a way of helping herself cope with hard times.

Flipping the Script
How I stopped putting myself down

(Excerpted from Hattie's Transitions diary)

March 23

My constant self-criticism is not only crippling my self-esteem but also damaging my ability to try new things.

This week, I wrote some more about how I put myself down. This time, I wrote down some of the terrible criticisms I heard as a child, like: Why you sitting here talking to the quiet b-tch?" and "I can't even sit next to her. Yo, shorty a straight weirdo."

I was shocked to remember that a girl in my class had the audacity to talk about me like that to my face. But writing down those insults surprised me because my feelings were less intense than I thought they would be, which was good. I even reread what I wrote, which I never do.

My journal writing left me in such good

spirits that I decided on the first action I would take to change: I decided that for the rest of the week, I'd tell myself good things anytime something negative happened. It worked—somewhat. If I started criticizing myself, I was able to stop and tell myself good things.

The problem was, I didn't believe a word that was coming out of my mouth. I truly felt like a compulsive liar. Despite telling myself all these good things, I still felt incompetent, deep down. But I think that I need to program my first thought to be positive, and eventually my feelings about myself might catch up.

April 6

Continuing with my theme of telling myself positive things, I planned this week to put Post-Its on my mirror with my positive characteristics written on each. That way, I'll wake up with good feelings about myself, and I'll be able to study my positive qualities. I also wrote an on-the-go list of my positive qualities in my journal so I'd always have it with me.

The list included: introspective, intelligent, considerate, understanding, timid, intuitive, intricate, broad-minded, caring, and able to disregard my emotions during times of stress.

April 13

This week I chose to write a story about a time in my life when I used all the positive characteristics I'd posted on my mirror. The story was a way to remind myself of my strength.

Here's what I wrote:

"When I was home with my mom, she refused to talk to me. In fact, she refused to talk to any of her family. (She has schizophrenia and was addicted to crack for years). Everyone else left her alone and ignored her crying.

"Although I was only 12, I was intelligent and intuitive enough to realize that my mom wasn't OK and needed help expressing herself. So instead of going to school, I was considerate and sensitive of her feelings—I stayed home with her every day.

"I wasn't sad to miss school. When I was younger, going to school was painful because I had only two outfits, my skin looked horrible, and my mom would mess up my hair. So you can imagine how much I got teased. (I am amazed I go to school today).

"That year I stayed home I was patient. I knew of my mom's violent nature, so I waited and eventually she opened up to me. She told me how she felt watched, and she pulled the blinds down. She told me that a boyfriend she'd had when she was 10 hypnotized her and was now having her watched.

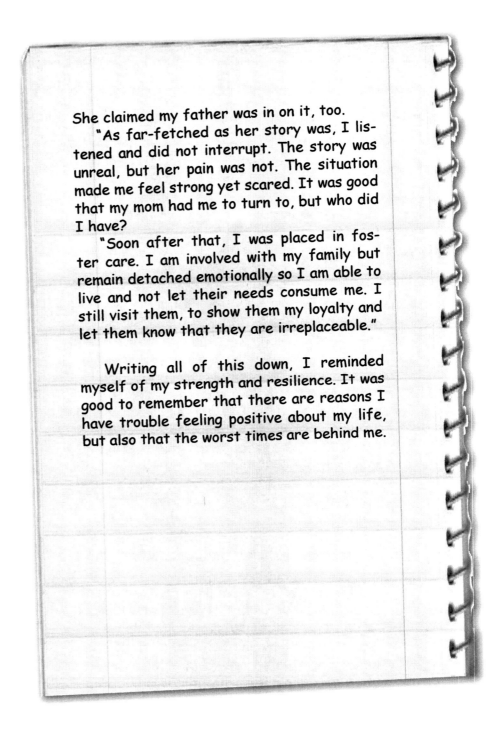

She claimed my father was in on it, too.

"As far-fetched as her story was, I listened and did not interrupt. The story was unreal, but her pain was not. The situation made me feel strong yet scared. It was good that my mom had me to turn to, but who did I have?

"Soon after that, I was placed in foster care. I am involved with my family but remain detached emotionally so I am able to live and not let their needs consume me. I still visit them, to show them my loyalty and let them know that they are irreplaceable."

Writing all of this down, I reminded myself of my strength and resilience. It was good to remember that there are reasons I have trouble feeling positive about my life, but also that the worst times are behind me.

Ask:

• *How did Hattie feel about herself at the beginning of the story?*

• *What kinds of strengths did she discover about herself?*

• *Can anyone think of additional strengths that Hattie shows in the story that she doesn't write about?*

• *The change that Hattie was working on was trying to stop putting herself down. What were the specific things she did to help her manage this transition? Did they help?*

Note: *Students may pick up on the fact that Hattie learns how to set boundaries for herself, and that she shows some self-awareness in understanding how she operates during times of stress by "shutting down" emotions. If not, you might suggest these things. It's also important to note that something might be a strength in one situation and not as helpful in another situation. For example, if Hattie shuts down emotionally too often, that can create other problems, like being unable to process her emotions or know what she's really feeling. One of the important lessons of the Transitions workshop is in learning how to pick the best tool for a given situation.*

Activity 4: Categorizing the Tools
(35 minutes)

 Tell the teens:

The specific things Hattie tried to help her stop putting herself down (like writing in a journal, using Post-It notes to remind herself of her positive qualities, etc.) are what we call "tools." In the Transitions Framework, tools are basically strategies— the things we do to help us cope with a change and all of the emotions that go along with it so that we feel more control over our lives. Today, you'll identify some

useful tools for managing transitions, starting with tools you already use.

• Ask teens to turn to the "Types of Tools" box on p. 40 in their journals. Explain that there are five major kinds of tools, and read the descriptions aloud together.

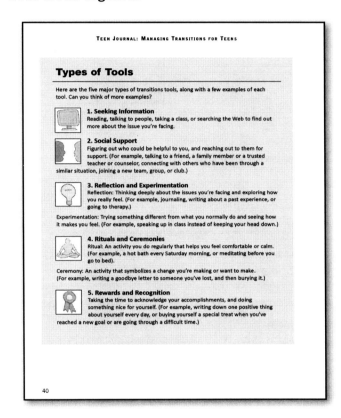

• Then, ask teens to turn the page to the "Tools in Action" sheet to see some specific examples of how other teens from the workshop used these kinds of tools. Ask for volunteers to read the testimonials aloud.

• Next, tell teens they're going to think about their own tools. Hand out several sticky notes to each teen. One each one, tell them to write down something they do or have done during times of change to help themselves manage transitions.

• On the board or a couple of sheets of flip chart paper, write down the five categories of

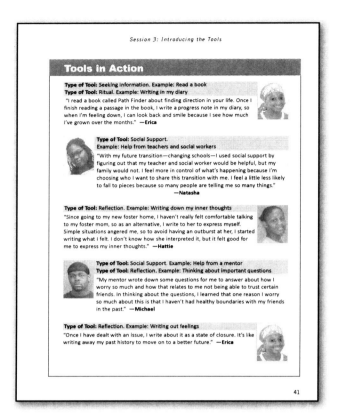

tools as listed at the top of the "My Personal Tool Bank" chart on p. 43 in the Teen Journal.

• Collect all the sticky notes and shuffle them. Then ask teens to turn to the My Personal Tool Bank worksheet (p. 43) in their journals.

• Read aloud the tools that the group came up with, and ask the group to call out which category each tool seems to fit with. Place the sticky notes in that category, and instruct teens to copy down each tool on the board in the appropriate category in their journals. The teens will note that some tools may fit into more than one category. That's fine. Either make duplicate stickies and put the tools in several categories, or choose the category that fits best.

• Tell teens that as they copy down each tool, they should think about whether it's something they have found useful or might like to try.

• Finally, ask teens to turn to the Tools Cheat

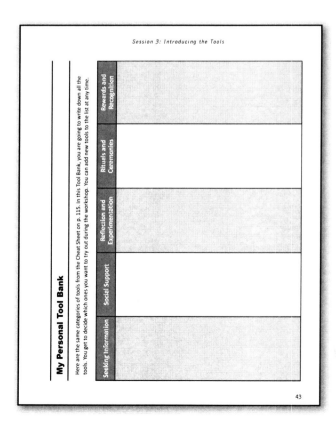

Sheet on p. 115 in their journals. Ask them to look at the tool examples in the boxes and pick a few that they might like to try. They should add the tools they'd like to try to their Personal Tool Bank page.

Note: If your group did not come up with any tools for one or more of the categories (or came up with very few tools for a particular category) make sure to highlight the tool examples for that category from the Cheat Sheet. Remind students that we all tend to rely on the same strategies, and that one thing they'll be doing in Part Two of this workshop is trying out some new and different strategies.

• Explain to teens that, in the next session, they will construct actual toolboxes, and will use them to store some of the tools that they want to try out in navigating their chosen transition. Tell them that they will have many opportunities to add tools to their toolboxes in the coming weeks.

• Assign homework: Tell teens that the toolbox they'll be making next week should be decorated in a way that reflects who they are. Encourage them to collect materials to personalize their toolboxes. In addition to magazine clippings and their own illustrations, suggest that they bring in favorite song lyrics, quotes, poems, etc., as well as personal mementos (photocopies or replicas are fine).

Closing Reflection (5 minutes)

Direct teens to the Closing Reflection section of their journals.

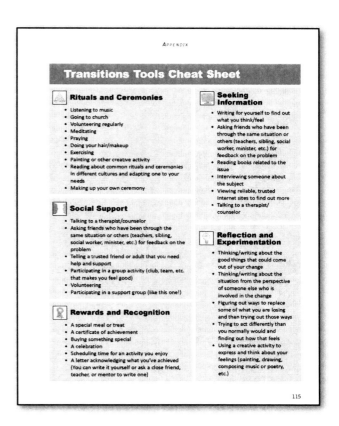

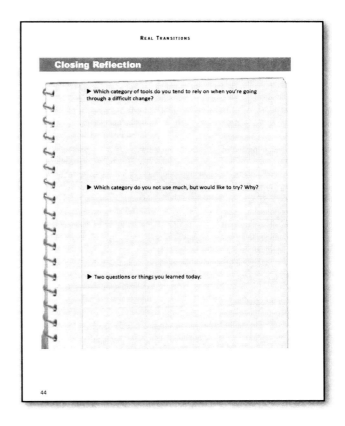

Session 4: Owning the Tools

Workshop Summary

Teens create their own physical toolboxes in order to reinforce awareness and understanding of a variety of tools, or strategies, so that they can effectively apply them to their own transition.

Time: 2 hours

Materials: Tool stencils (copied from pp. 57-59 in this guide), cardstock, toolbox construction/decoration materials (boxes, markers, magazines, scissors, glue, etc.), sample decorated toolbox (See Note, p. 60).

Note: The physical "toolbox" can be as simple as a shoebox with a string for a handle, or you can get boxes made with handles. (For one session we used inexpensive cardboard hat boxes.) If your resources are thin, don't be afraid to improvise! Any box will do.

Goals:

1. Teens will internalize concepts of Transitions tools and stages by constructing a personalized toolbox.
2. Teens will feel increased ownership for Transitions tools.
3. Teens will identify tools they already use and new tools they want to use in managing their own transitions.

Activity 1: M&Ms Check-In (10 minutes)

See description in Session 3.

Activity 2: Constructing the Tools (45 minutes)

Note: In advance of the session, make copies of the tools on pp. 57-59 in this guide and cut them out so teens can use them as stencils.

• Tell teens to turn to the "My Personal Tool Bank" sheet in their journals from Session 3 (p. 43).

Session 3: Introducing the Tools

My Personal Tool Bank

Here are the same categories of tools from the Cheat Sheet on p. 115. In this Tool Bank, you are going to write down all the tools. You get to decide which ones you want to try out during the workshop. You can add new tools to the list at any time.

Seeking Information | Social Support | Reflection and Experimentation | Rituals and Ceremonies | Rewards and Recognition

43

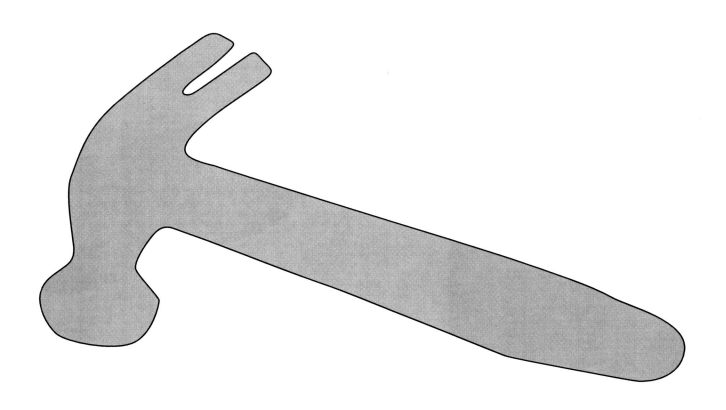

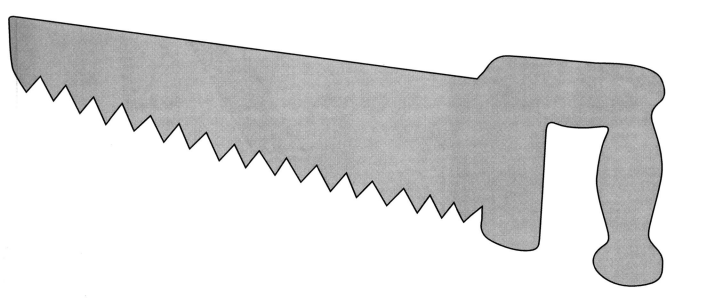

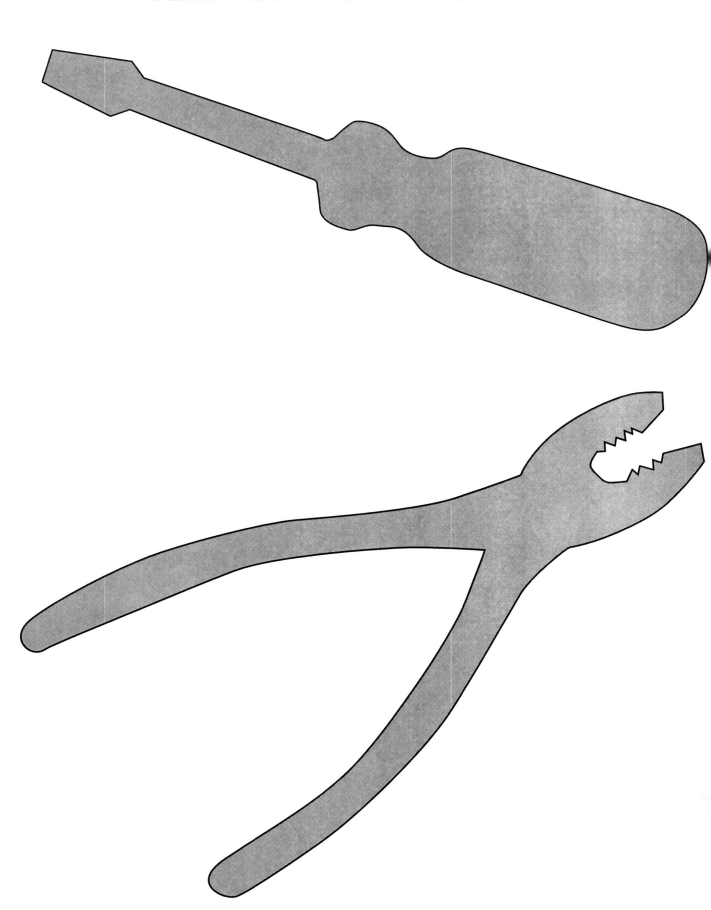

Tell the teens:

Last week, we created our own Tool Banks that listed all of the tool categories and tools that we could think of. We also saw that a single tool can fall into more than one category.

Today, you're going to make your own toolbox—an actual box of tools you've already listed on the Tool Bank sheet along with new ones you pick up along the way. (Remember, whenever you discover a new tool that you like, add it to the Tool Bank.)

The point of making your own toolbox is to help you become really familiar with these tools, so that when you're working on your transition, you'll have a lot of options to try.

Did anyone think of new tools since our last session? (Pause. Probe.)

As you personalize your toolbox, feel free to share tool ideas with each other so that everyone learns new, effective ways of making change and managing transitions.

• Pass out the tool-shaped stencils, scissors, and cardstock paper. Teens will trace and cut out several tool-shaped objects using the stencils.

On one side of the tool-shaped cardstock paper, they will write the name of a category of tools. On the other side, they'll describe one tool from this category that they use or would like to try, using their "My Personal Tool Bank" worksheet and "Tools Cheat Sheet" as resources.

Encourage teens to discuss and exchange tool ideas with one another to supplement their own tried-and-true tools.

Activity 3: Personalizing the toolbox
(60 minutes)

Note: The best way to approach this activity is for you the facilitator to decorate a simple model toolbox based on your own experiences and bring it to this session to share with teens. It should reflect your personality, your life transitions, and your feelings about those transitions. This will allow teens to get to know you and build trust, and it will help them get started with this part of the activity.

Pass out shoeboxes (or whatever containers you've chosen to use for the teens' toolboxes) and collage materials. Explain that they'll use these as toolboxes to store the tools they've just created.

To start, they'll personalize their toolboxes by creating a collage on the outside. They can use photos, poems or song lyrics, pictures from magazines, words, or phrases that symbolize changes they've made in the past and/or changes they'd like to make in the future, and things that have helped them deal with change (including their own strengths).

• With or without a model, emphasize that personalizing the toolbox means much more than decorating it: encourage teens to reach beyond "advertising" their favorite music, brands, etc., and prompt them to think about what those things mean to them, and what they say about their personality and their approach to change. The teens can be as creative as they wish, but the point is for them to express their experiences and feelings about transitions—past, present and future.

• During the last 10 minutes of this activity, give teens the chance to share their toolboxes with the group if they'd like to. Make sure teens put the tools they've cut out into their toolboxes, and find a safe place to store them—you'll be using these again in upcoming weeks.

Closing Reflection (5 minutes)

Direct teens to the Closing Reflection section of their journals.

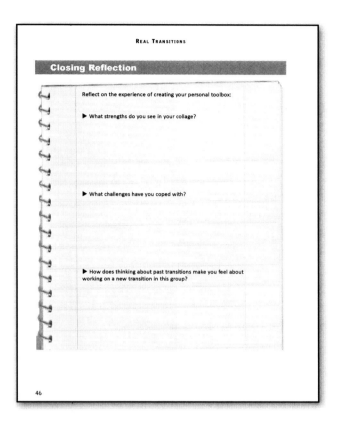

Session 5: Stages of Transition—Letting Go

Workshop Summary

Teens will review the three stages of Transition and focus on the first one, Letting Go. They will create a timeline of significant changes from their own lives.

Time: 2 hours

Materials: Board/flipchart, markers, pens

Goals:

1. Participants will learn about the characteristics, emotions and tools associated with the Letting Go stage.
2. Participants will recognize the importance of acknowledging the losses that come with any change.
3. Participants will learn that you have to let go of some past entanglements to move forward with your emotional life.

Activity 1: M&Ms Check-In (10 minutes)

See description in Session 3.

Activity 2: Review the Stages
(10 minutes)

Ask teens to turn to the Transitions chart on p. 48 in their journals, and review it with the group. Point out that in this chart, as you move from left to right, the stages overlap. That's because in real life, as you work through a transition, you probably won't move neatly from one stage to the next. When you're mostly in the Chaos stage, you might still be doing a little work on Letting Go. When you're in New Start, you might still have some days when you feel thrown back into Chaos—and that's OK.

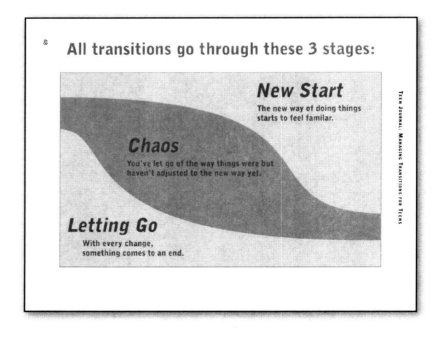

All transitions go through these 3 stages:

New Start
The new way of doing things starts to feel familar.

Chaos
You've let go of the way things were but haven't adjusted to the new way yet.

Letting Go
With every change, something comes to an end.

TEEN JOURNAL: MANAGING TRANSITIONS FOR TEENS

Tell the teens:

For the remaining sessions in this first half of the workshop we'll be exploring these three stages in more depth.

In the second half of the workshop, you'll use what you've learned about the stages of transition and the tools to work on your own transition.

So over the next three sessions, start thinking about a transition that you'd like to focus on. It could be related to a change in schools, jobs, relationships, or even how you feel about yourself. You won't have to decide until Session 9, but you can start thinking about ideas now.

Activity 3: Introducing the Letting Go Stage (30 minutes)

Tell the teens:

Today we'll be focusing on the first stage, Letting Go. You'll learn the symptoms and feelings of this stage. You'll also identify tools that are especially helpful in dealing with feelings associated with Letting Go.

• Instruct teens to turn to the "Letting Go" page in their journals (p. 5). Tell them that this is a kind of "cheat sheet" they will use throughout the workshop series to understand stages of change (there are similar pages for Chaos and New Start).

• Briefly read through the *description* of the Letting Go stage (in the box) and the *emotions* it can provoke (the words above the sidewalk). You can note to teens that not everyone goes through all of these emotions during the Letting Go stage,

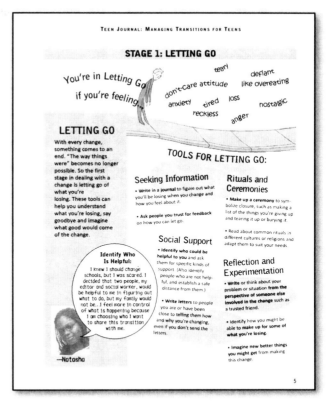

and some people experience emotions that are not on this worksheet—but it's still a good guide.

• Ask teens to call out a few typical changes (e.g., moving to a new foster home, starting a new job). For each one, brainstorm together what a person might be *losing* when they make that change, and note those losses on the board or chart paper. Make sure to talk about a few "positive" changes to emphasize the point that even when you make a positive change, you are losing something, and it's important to acknowledge that.

For example, you might be thrilled to be leaving a foster home and moving into an apartment on your own. But you'll be losing the experience and familiarity of living with other people (even if you didn't like them) and of not having to worry about bills and rent. You might be losing the experience of feeling like a child. It's good to be aware of these possible losses.

• Finally, read through the suggested *tools* for Letting Go. Then ask teens if they would suggest any other tools for this stage, based on tools they've included in their Tool Bank.

Emphasize that the tools for the Letting Go stage are meant to help you understand and express your feelings about whatever you're losing in a change—not prevent those feelings or push them away.

Note that Letting Go is the stage that people tend to try to skip over—nobody wants to feel sad or linger over their losses. But acknowledging what you're losing and how you feel about it is the only way you'll eventually be able to move on.

Activity 4: Timeline of Your Life
(60 minutes)

[OR Learning How to Let Go, p. 106. See note below.]

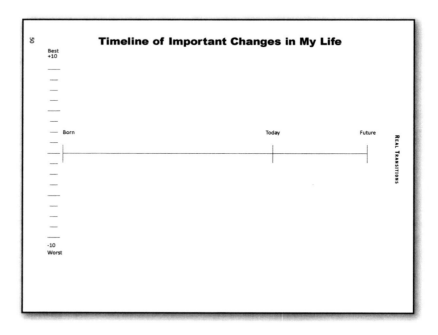

Note: *If your group is particularly inclined toward reading and writing, you can use an alternate activity, Learning How to Let Go, in place of (or in addition to) the timeline. That activity, on p. 106 in this guide, involves reading stories by teens who are struggling with the Letting Go stage, and working in small groups to identify and write about what the characters are losing and how they might cope.*

• Ask participants to turn to page 49 in their journals, and take turns reading aloud the instructions for making a "Timeline of Your Life."

• Give them about 45 minutes to create their timelines and answer the reflection questions on the following page in their journals.

• Then ask for volunteers to share any things that stood out to them about this activity (note that they do not have to share their timelines or talk about specific events). What did they notice about how they dealt with changes in the past, and how different changes affected them? Did anything surprise them?

Note: *Many youth in care have experienced multiple traumatic losses. Those previous experiences can make acknowledging current losses difficult—even if the loss is small, or even if the teen wants to let go of something that's negative.*

This is a complicated idea for many teens—that past experiences affect our emotional responses to current changes in our lives. And, even more importantly, we're often not aware that this is happening. Our responses are unconscious.

When we're responding to current changes based on old emotions, and especially when those emotions are unconscious, they can control us, instead of us controlling them.

The timeline activity is a good way to introduce this idea and ask teens to think about how their reactions to change may be affected by these past experiences.

Closing Reflection (10 minutes)

Direct teens to the Closing Reflection section of their journals.

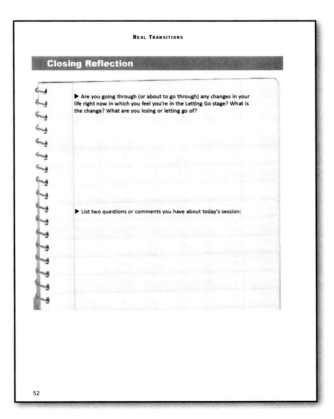

REAL TRANSITIONS

Closing Reflection

► Are you going through (or about to go through) any changes in your life right now in which you feel you're in the Letting Go stage? What is the change? What are you losing or letting go of?

► List two questions or comments you have about today's session:

52

Session 6: Stages of Transition—Chaos

Workshop Summary

Teens learn about the emotions and tools associated with the Chaos stage, and read and discuss a story that exemplifies this stage.

Time: 2 hours

Materials: Board, markers, pens

Goals:

1. Teens will understand the Chaos stage as the confusing time between letting go of familiar habits and setting new goals.
2. Teens will understand and name the emotions often associated with the Chaos stage. They will understand in particular that feelings of anxiety and confusion are normal.
3. Teens will be able to name and describe tools they can use to survive the Chaos stage.

Activity 1: M&Ms Check-in (10 minutes)

See description in Session 3, p. 46.

Activity 2: Introduction to Chaos stage (20 minutes)

 Tell the teens:

Today we're going to continue to learn about the stages of transition. Last time, we learned about the first stage—Letting Go. This time, we're going to learn about the middle stage—Chaos.

Does anyone want to share what they think of when they hear the word "chaos?"

Teens may say things like confusion, doubt, craziness, etc. Note to teens that even though chaos might seem bewildering and scary, when things are disorderly or undefined there is also a sense of possibility, and opportunities to establish new patterns and habits, which can be positive things.

Write teens' responses and your additions on the board.

• Instruct teens to turn to the "Chaos" sheet in their journals (p. 6). Briefly read through the description of the Chaos stage (in the box) and the emotions it can provoke (the words above the sidewalk). Emphasize that not everyone goes through all of these emotions during the Chaos stage, and some people experience emotions that are not mentioned, which is normal. Ask teens which emotions on the sheet are positive, which are negative, and which could be both.

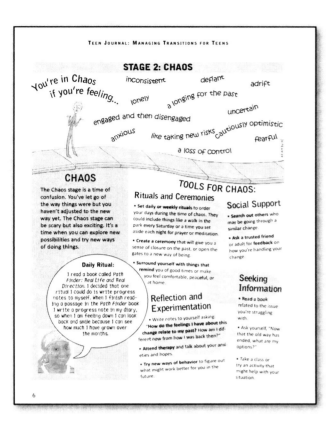

• Finally, read through the suggested tools for Chaos. Then ask teens if they would suggest any other tools for this stage, based on things they've written so far in their Tool Bank.

Activity 3: Reflecting on Chaos
(20 minutes)

• Ask teens to turn to the "Reflecting on Chaos" worksheet in their journals (p. 54) and read the instructions aloud together. Give teens about 10 minutes to write. Then, ask for volunteers to call out some of the strengths and tools they wrote down (they do not have to explain the particular situation they wrote about). Keep track of the strengths and tools volunteered on the board.

Activity 4: Story: "Manning Up"
(30 minutes)

 Tell the teens:

We've come up with a lot of good ideas for how to help ourselves work through the Chaos stage and manage our emotions. Now we're going to see if we can use these resources to help another teen who's struggling through the Chaos stage.

We're going to read a story about Chris, who has just found out that he's going to become a parent, and whose baby is due a few days after he turns 21 and ages out of foster care. So he has a lot of new things to get used to and a lot to figure out.

• Ask for volunteers to take turns reading "Manning Up" by Christopher Guzman, (p. 55 in their journals, p. 68 in this guide).

Christopher Guzman

Manning Up
I age out the same month my baby is born. Gulp.

By Christopher Guzman

I was chilling at my godparents' house when I got the text from my girl Corrie. It had a picture attached that I didn't understand, so I texted her back, "wwwhhh-haaaaatttttt?" Her next text said, "Negative is the straight line; positive is the plus sign." I looked back at the picture: a plastic stick with a plus sign.

I knew her period was late, but now it was real. I threw my phone in the air and laughed and yelled at the same time. I was scared but also amazed that I was bringing a life into the world. I couldn't believe this was happening to me.

We didn't intend to get pregnant, but I don't believe in abortion. I asked Corrie what she wanted to do, and she told me that she doesn't believe in abortion either. She said, "I'm going to leave it in; we're going to have a family."

So I'm going to be a father. I don't know much about what's going to happen, but I know I don't want to do what my father did—he left my family the day I was born. He just walked out and left a letter to my mom saying, "I'm not ready to be a father to three boys. PEACE." He moved to Puerto Rico to make a whole new foundation, including starting another family. That hurt. He didn't see me before he left, but it still feels like a personal rejection.

Me as a Father

I feel like a kid in a kid's body, partly because I'm short, and also because I'm only 20 and haven't even aged out of care yet. I need a job and a place to live. I don't really feel ready to be a father. I feel more stress than ever imagining what it will be like when the baby is born. I know it's going to be stressful when the baby wakes up early in the morning, needs changing, needs feeding. It's hard for me to deal with new things that I'm not used to. Knowing that I'm not ready makes it more difficult to hear family members, friends and associates say, "You're not ready! How are you going to pay for this? Where are you going to live?" It's too much.

I need to get a job to support my child. I need money for rent and health insurance and to take the baby to the hospital if it's sick, to buy baby food and clothes. There's so much I don't know about a baby, but I do know that responsibility comes first.

To be a father, I have to change my life and become a better person because I've been a knucklehead. I've been hanging around with my friends—smoking, drinking, partying, doing what normal teenagers do. In August my life will change completely: the baby is due, and I turn 21 and age out of care.

I'd like to worry less, but I have more to worry about than ever. Becoming a father is the hardest and scariest thing that I can think of besides going to war.

How Do I Learn This Stuff?

I didn't have a father to look up to who could understand what I was going through. I had role models and father figures, but no one can replace a father growing up. I always wanted what someone else had because there was no one to buy things for me or take me to the movies. Even after I turned 18, I still missed having a father. I wish that I'd had a father to talk to when I needed some advice about things that I don't know—including being a father!

I don't want my child growing up like I did. That's why I'm going to give my baby what my father didn't give to me: guidance, encouragement, strength, hope, and the most important, love.

Taking Care of Others

I've made a good start by going with Corrie to her doctor's appointments. The day that I went to the first ultrasound was the happiest day ever. I saw my baby for the first time as an embryo. I was proud of myself for playing the role and stepping up.

Corrie was in a lot of pain during the ultrasound. I was holding her hand throughout it. I told her "Baby, you're OK, everything's going to be OK," letting her know that we're in this together. I felt like a husband holding his wife through the pain and struggles.

While the nurse was taking the pictures of the baby I was asking her very important questions about the baby, but she ignored me! I was shocked. Corrie asked a question and the nurse answered her. I got very offended.

I wanted to smack fire out of the nurse. But I calmed down. I was proud of holding my temper because it showed me that I'm not quitting for anything. I'm already doing more than my father ever did. I got a book about pregnancy and I've been reading about the growth of the baby, how it looks, how much it should weigh, and things like that.

Afterward, I was walking home just looking at the picture of the baby I'd taken on my phone and I started crying again. I cried every emotion, but mostly I was scared about the responsibility and happy because I'm bringing another human being into this world.

Me and Corrie

Corrie and I have a good connection, but things have changed since we found out about the baby. We barely speak to each other or see each other anymore. I call her and we only talk about the baby and what we're going to do and stuff. We used to joke around more. Things are more serious now, not fun.

We're losing a part of each other because of the baby. We're losing love because things aren't the way they used to be. She's tired and nauseous and I've been tired and worried about where we're going to live. I need help with everything.

We're going to be One no matter what, but now we're not One, feelings-wise. I told her that I was worried that we were drifting apart, that we barely kiss or converse. She said, "Sorry that it's happening like this; it will get better." I said, "Whatever."

I wonder how it would be if we were not having a baby. Sometimes I wonder if she would have broken up with me by now. She was on me to get a job even before she got pregnant.

Family

Corrie's dad died when she was young, and she's very close to her mother. She has a sister who also had a baby last year. Corrie's mother and cousins and aunts and grandmother fight over who gets to babysit that baby.

I wish I had a mother like that and I'm glad for the support. But sometimes it seems like I have to prove myself to Corrie's mother. I look for jobs and apartments every day, but Corrie and her mother act like I'm not trying hard enough. They'll ask, "Well, why didn't you do this or do that?" It makes me feel like they don't believe me, like they're asking for proof of what I do all day.

Corrie doesn't like any of the names I've picked for the baby. I wanted my friend to be the godmother, but Corrie chose someone else. I want my kid to eat chicken and meat, and Corrie's already decided the baby will be a vegetarian.

An apartment below her mother's apartment might become available, and if we live there, I know her mother will be making a lot of the decisions about the baby. I worry that if I don't get a job or get into school or get a place to live soon that they'll only treat me like the baby-father, not the father.

But I want to be the father. I want to wake up every day and strive to provide for my child. I've accepted that this baby is what matters most now, more than all of my fears and the obstacles in my past.

Even though I don't have parents, I have people who will help. My godparents will be like grandparents. I know that they will help me in any way possible. They took me in after I left from a group home upstate and accepted me into the family.

I'm also glad to have my friends Kalid, Marc, and Dre, even though Dre moved to Texas last year. He and I always joked around calling each other "son" and "my child." When I told him Corrie was pregnant, he said "Wow, I'm going to become a grandfather," and we both laughed. I asked all three of those guys to be godfather to my baby. They said that they were happy to be a part of the baby's life and that they'd be there for us 100 percent.

August

I turn 21 and age out on August 5. What turning 21 means is losing all the money I got for school, for clothes, food, housing, transportation, haircuts, everything. My baby is due August 22, and I have to be there to take care of it. I want my baby to have birth parents, not be part of the system.

Now my responsibility is to become a good father. I'm getting up every day to look for jobs and internships and colleges that will accept a special education diploma (which is really a certificate that says I completed high school). I also study on my own time just to stay on track with my education.

I'm going to take a fatherhood class to prepare me to become a successful father. I'm still afraid because we're in a recession, and how am I going to find a job if nobody's hiring? But even though it's hard, I won't stop trying because somebody is depending on me now to live a successful life.

Activity 5: Chaos Discussion (30 minutes)

• Divide the group into pairs, and ask them to turn to the "Finding Our Way Through Chaos" worksheet on p. 62 in their journals.

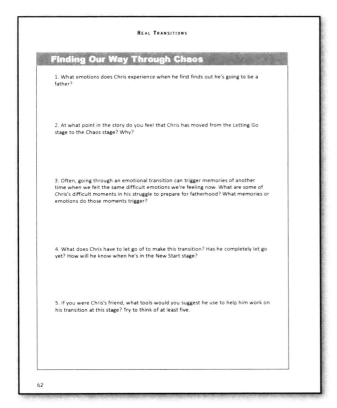

Closing Reflection (10 minutes)

Direct teens to the Closing Reflection section of their journals.

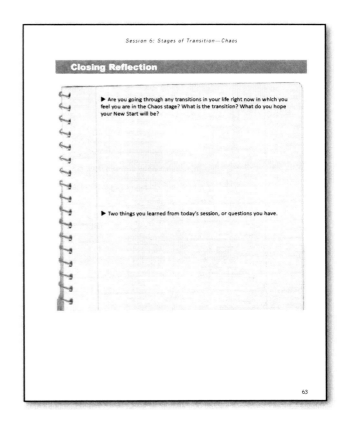

Tell the pairs to discuss together the responses to each question. Emphasize that they do not need to agree on their responses, but should discuss why they think the way they do. Circulate during this activity to ensure that teens are engaged with one another in discussion.

• Give the pairs about 15 minutes to complete the worksheet questions. Then, read each question aloud and have volunteers share their responses.

Emphasize, again, that responses may vary. The point here is to get teens to identify the author's strengths and challenges and identify tools that may be useful in helping him complete his transition.

Session 7: Stages of Transition—New Start

Workshop Summary

Teens will learn about the New Start stage and invent a realistic continuation of the fairytale Cinderella. They will then focus on their own goals for the rest of the workshop and beyond.

Time: 2 hours

Materials: Whiteboard/flipchart, blank paper, pens, masking tape, M&Ms, copies of worksheet questionnaire (copied from p. 80).

Goals:

1. Teens will understand the characteristics, emotions, and tools associated with the New Start stage of transition.
2. Teens will recognize the circular nature of transition as they explore the idea that New Start is not the same as a static ending.
3. Teens will demonstrate and reflect on what they've learned about the Transitions process.

Note: This session marks the end of Part One. Although it's not built into the two-hour lesson schedule, we recommend adding a ceremonial element to this session to celebrate your group's progress. You may want to involve the teens in this process by asking them in the previous workshop session what they would like; this might include a special meal or dessert, certificates, etc.

Activity 1: M&Ms Check-In (15 minutes)

In addition to the usual check-in, you may want to take this opportunity to ask teens to reflect briefly on what they've learned or discovered in the workshop so far, and what they're feeling about the second half. (See p. 46 for a description of the M&Ms check-in.)

Activity 2: Introduction to New Start (15 minutes)

 Tell the teens:

> *We've spent the past couple weeks talking about the first two stages of transition: Letting Go and Chaos. Today, as we finish off the first half of our workshop, we're going to look ahead to the final stage, New Start.*

• Instruct teens to turn to New Start page in their journals (p. 7). Briefly read through the description of the New Start stage (in the box) and the emotions it can provoke (the words above the sidewalk). Emphasize that not everyone goes through all of these emotions during the New Start stage, and some people experience emotions that are not mentioned, which is normal. Ask teens which emotions on the sheet are positive, which are negative, and which could be both.

Activity 3: Cinderella's New Start
(30 minutes)

• Instruct teens to turn to the "Cinderella's New Start" worksheet in their journals (p. 66) and read it aloud.

• Give teens about 20 minutes to write, then ~~answer~~ the questions together. Call on volun-
Tell the teens:

> *The point of this activity is to remind you that change is inevitable and will continue throughout our lives. That means we'll continue to work through transitions. That's why it's called a new start instead of an ending.*

> *And even when we make a new start that feels positive and we see progress, there will still be reminders of difficult things from our past that we have to face from time to time, especially as we*

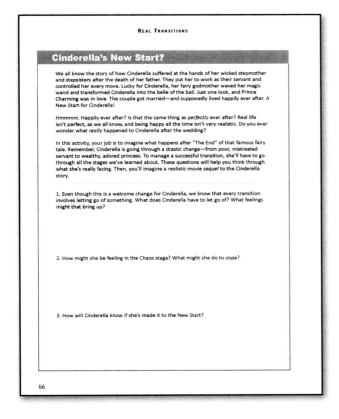

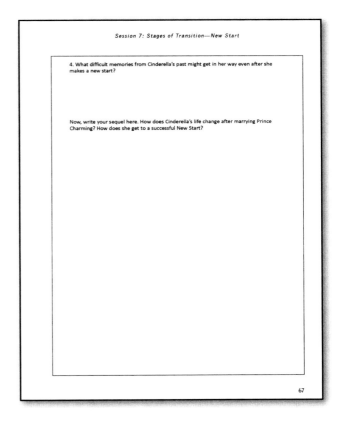

encounter new changes. So we have to keep working on the things that get in our way.

teers to share their update stories.

Activity 4: Thinking About Your Transition (35 minutes)

• Ask students to turn to the "Thinking About Your Transition" page in their journals (p. 68) and read the first three paragraphs aloud together. As teens complete the worksheet, circulate around

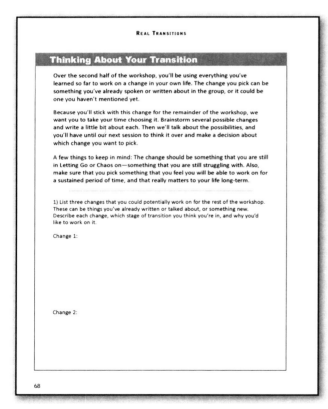

REAL TRANSITIONS

Thinking About Your Transition

Over the second half of the workshop, you'll be using everything you've learned so far to work on a change in your own life. The change you pick can be something you've already spoken or written about in the group, or it could be one you haven't mentioned yet.

Because you'll stick with this change for the remainder of the workshop, we want you to take your time choosing it. Brainstorm several possible changes and write a little bit about each. Then we'll talk about the possibilities, and you'll have until our next session to think it over and make a decision about which change you want to pick.

A few things to keep in mind: The change should be something that you are still in Letting Go or Chaos on—something that you are still struggling with. Also, make sure that you pick something that you feel you will be able to work on for a sustained period of time, and that really matters to your life long-term.

1) List three changes that you could potentially work on for the rest of the workshop. These can be things you've already written or talked about, or something new. Describe each change, which stage of transition you think you're in, and why you'd like to work on it.

Change 1:

Change 2:

68

the room and confer with students. Check to make sure they are choosing changes that seem manageable.

If possible, it's a good idea to build in time here or after the session to meet privately with

each student and discuss their potential change and transition process in more detail. This will help teens refine their ideas and give you a better sense of what they want to work on in Part Two, and what the potential challenges might be.

Make sure to talk with teens about any goals that seem unrealistic or overly challenging (e.g., "I want to fix my relationship with my mom,") or too vague (e.g., "I want to be better person," or "I want to be independent."). The more you can help students think through the process now, the easier it will be for them to select an appropriate change to work on in the next session.

Activity 5: Affirmations (15 minutes)

 Tell the teens:

We are now halfway through our workshop. In the next session, we'll start working on our individual changes and supporting each other through that transition process. So before we leave today, we're going to take a few minutes to appreciate one another.

This is what you'll do: Walk around and write down something positive about each person on the piece of paper that's taped to their back, without identifying yourself.

You can write something simple— some positive adjectives that describe the person, something good you think about when you see them, some important contribution they've made to the group, etc. Just keep it short and 100% positive.

• Pass out paper and masking tape. Ask each student to tape a piece of paper on to the back of the person sitting next to them.

• Give teens about 10 minutes to circulate. After everyone has written something on everyone else's sheet, have teens remove the sheets from their backs and read what the other group members had to say about them. This is a nice, affirming way to end the first seven weeks and motivate them to return for the next session after the break.

Note: There may be some students who are uncomfortable with the physical proximity involved in this activity. If that's the case, you may wish to modify this activity by providing the option of writing that teen's affirming statements on index cards that each teen returns to you, and which you then affix to a larger paper and present to the teen. But most teens will enjoy this tactile activity—and the chance to let everyone see his/her affirming statements.

Closing Reflection (10 minutes)

In place of the regular closing reflection in their journals, pass out copies of the Transitions Workshop Questionnaire (copy them from the next page) and ask teens to complete them.

Emphasize that they do not need to write their names on the questionnaire, and that you will use their feedback to try to make the workshop as helpful as possible for everyone. Make sure teens drop off the questionnaires before they leave the session.

Note: If there will be a break of more than one week in between this session and when students return for Part Two, make sure to go over the schedule. Let teens know if you will be contacting them to remind them of when the next session starts and make sure you have their updated email addresses and phone numbers.

Transitions Workshop Questionnaire

(This is your closing reflection for today)

We'd like your feedback! Please take a few minutes to thoughtfully complete these statements. Be honest—everything you tell us will be confidential, anonymous, and very useful for making positive changes to the way we do things in the next 8 sessions!

What I liked best about the first half of the Transitions workshop was:

What I'd like to see change in Part 2 is:

How I felt about sharing my problems in the group was:

Other comments (use back if necessary):

Looking Ahead: A Few Thoughts for Group Leaders About Endings

At this halfway point, it's important to look ahead to the next nine sessions and think about how best to acknowledge the teens' accomplishments, as well as how to prepare them for the inevitable end of the workshop.

You will likely find that teens have many ways of processing the realization that the workshop is going to end. Some may start skipping sessions, stop participating during sessions, or stop coming altogether; others may act out in ways that jeopardize their continued participation in the workshop, as a way of rejecting the group before they get rejected (i.e., the feeling of abandonment that may come as the workshop ends). These are all typical reactions.

It's important to talk periodically about those feelings as a group, and it's a good opportunity to remind your teens that what they're experiencing is a normal part of anticipating change and managing a transition—just as we've been discussing all these weeks. It's also important to talk privately with any teens whose behaviors indicate that they're struggling with this impending change.

About halfway through the second half of the workshop series, be sure to introduce the idea that the workshop will be ending on a specific date. Reiterate that mixed feelings are normal, and invite your teens to share ways that they might remain a support system for each other even after they're no longer meeting in the group.

This is also a chance to remind them of what they're gaining by inviting them to be part of the planning of their "graduation" from the Transitions program. It's ideal to include the teens in the planning process so that they have something to look forward to even though the workshop is ending. (Involving them in the planning process will also help them feel more in control of this ending.)

Some ideas for planning a modest graduation ceremony are included on p. 103.

PART II
Transitions in Action

SESSIONS 8-16

Students will choose one change from their own lives that they would like to work on. Each week, they will pick a new tool to try. They will report back on how it went, discuss their progress with the group, and give each other feedback. The last session is a celebration or graduation ceremony.

Note to Facilitators:
Handling Emotions in Part Two

The second half of the workshop is a big shift. Teens move from learning to action: Now that they've become familiar with the Transitions framework, they get the chance to try out the process on a change in their own lives. And the format of the sessions changes too. Instead of reading and other activities, teens will spend each session writing and discussing their progress.

For the teens in your group, this process will inevitably touch on past experiences of change and bring up some strong emotions. As the facilitator, you can help teens feel safe by maintaining clear expectations and boundaries in the group, and watching out for when teens seem in over their heads. Here are a few tips:

• Try to keep discussion focused on the tools and what teens have found useful and not useful. Don't let a particular teen's issue dominate the group or cause a session to run over time (a few minutes is OK; an hour is problematic.) If a teen has had a difficult week or is particularly upset during a session, be supportive and solicit the support of the group, but don't feel that the issue needs to be "solved" before the discussion can move on. If you feel that a teen needs more help or attention, approach him or her privately after the session and offer to talk further.

• Pay attention to signs that a student is having trouble (skipping sessions, "acting out," withdrawing from the group, etc.). Try to point out these behaviors to the teen one-on-one, in a non-confrontational way. Express your concern and work with the teen to find ways to make the workshop feel more manageable. In particular, pay careful attention to the tools teens are choosing each week and help steer teens away from tools that seem wildly unrealistic, overwhelming, or unsafe.

• Make sure to run the "personal ground rules" and boundaries activities in session 9, and refer back to them as needed. Remind teens that they are in control of what they share.

• Remind students that transition is a gradual process, and that it's hard. Help teens set realistic goals in session 8, and keep reminding them that "success" means trying new coping strategies and learning from them—not necessarily solving all of their problems.

• Get help when needed. If you're concerned that a teen is in danger or needs more help than you can give, consult with a colleague or your supervisor.

Session 8: Identifying Your Change

Workshop Summary

Teens will choose the change they want to focus on in the second half of the workshop and preview the process by reading a Transitions diary.

Time: 2 hours

Materials: Teen Journal and Leader's Guide

Goals:

1. Teens will understand that a successful transition does not necessarily mean reaching every goal.
2. Teens will recognize the importance of self-discovery in the process of transition and the value of using that to make successful future transitions.
3. Teens will be aware that past experiences can influence the success of a transition and consider strategies to avoid dwelling in past perceived failures and painful experiences.
4. Teens will continue building trust and supportive communication skills as they discuss their transition with the group.

Activity 1: M&Ms Check-In (10 minutes)

If your group had a break after the first half of the workshop, use this time to ask teens to report back at least one thing they did over the break, one thing that's stuck with them from the first half of the workshop, and how they're feeling about starting up again. (See p. 46 for a description of the M&Ms check-in.)

Activity 2: Choosing Your Change (25 minutes)

 Tell the teens:

Today it's finally time to officially choose the change that you intend to work on for the second half of the workshop.

REAL TRANSITIONS

Choosing Your Change

1. YOUR CHANGE: Please state the change you will work on for the next six weeks. (If this is not one of the changes you wrote about in the last session, make sure to describe it in detail, including what stage you think you're in now, what you will be losing, what concerns you have, and why you'd like to work on this change.)

The change I'm going to work on is:

2. GOALS FOR MY TRANSITION: Please write down a short, specific list of the goals you want to achieve with this transition. What are *specific* feelings you would like to understand better? What are *specific* behaviors you want to change or try out? What are *specific, reasonable* goals you want to aim for in the next few months?

74

• Ask teens to look back at the three changes and related transitions they wrote about in the last session (Journal p. 68) and pick the one they'd like to work on for the next six weeks.

Then, direct them to the "Choosing Your Change" worksheet on p. 74. Read aloud the instructions aloud together, then have teens complete the exercise.

Explain that after they complete their worksheets, each student will meet with you individually to talk through their change and finalize their choice.

As they write, you can circulate to ensure teens are differentiating between change and transition in their responses, and that their expressed change is focused and manageable.

Activity 3: Reading a Transitions Diary
(45 minutes)

 Tell the teens:

To prepare you for the process of going through the change and transition you've just described, we're going to read the story "School Daze," which is the actual week-by-week account of Natasha's journey through the Transitions workshop.

Natasha shows how she handled the transition process. It will help you get you thinking about common feelings associated with change, and about the tools that might be helpful for managing your transition.

While you read and discuss the story with each other, I'm going to ask each of you to meet with me individually to go over the change you chose.

Planning Your Transition

Now that you've chosen your change, it's time to start thinking about your plan for working through it. Today, we're going to read "School Daze," the story of how Natasha used this workshop and the tools to help her get through a big change: going to a new school.

This change brought up all kinds of difficult emotions and memories for Natasha. She tried some tools that worked, and others that didn't. In the end, Natasha was not sure if she really achieved the goal she made for herself at the beginning of the workshop. But going through the process, she did make positive progress (Natasha went on to college and is doing well, even though she still has her ups and downs).

As you read Natasha's story, keep your own chosen change in mind. Though your transition may be different than hers, notice the things she says that you connect with: feelings, actions, patterns, habits, etc.

Afterward, you'll think about the questions on p. 85 and discuss them with a partner. You should each take turns answering every question. It's OK to say that you are not comfortable answering a question or are not sure.

75

• Break the group into pairs, and direct everyone to turn to the "Planning Your Transition" page in their journals (p. 75). Read the instructions aloud together.

• Next, describe or write on the board the order that teens will meet with you in. (You can go around the circle, go alphabetically, etc.) Pick a spot where you will confer with teens (ideally outside the room). Direct everyone to begin reading Natasha's story to themselves while you begin the teen meetings. After they finish reading, each pair should discuss the questions on p. 85.

Note: If you have a co-facilitator, he or she should remain in the room and help teens complete the Partner Questions activity. If not, check in with the group periodically to make sure they are staying on task.

With each teen, review their chosen change and make sure it seems realistic and manageable. Ask what concerns they have about managing this transition and what they hope to accomplish.

What are some of the tools they could imagine using? Try to help them adjust their change as necessary to make it more specific or more manageable.

Remember—teens may not choose to work on the change you think is most important for them, and that's OK. The point is for teens to think about how to manage a transition in real life, and experiment with some strategies. Hopefully, they will take what they've learned and be able to apply it to other, perhaps more difficult changes in their lives after the workshop is over.

Activity 4: What Does Success Mean? (15 minutes)

Once you have met with each participant and everyone has completed the partner questions, call the group back together and review the last two questions (about what Natasha got out of the program, and if it's possible to achieve success even if you don't reach your goal in the workshop).

Emphasize that most transitions will not get neatly resolved within the next six weeks. The point is to try out new ways of thinking and acting and see if there are ways that you can feel more in control of changes that are happening in your life.

Our hope is that, through this process, participants will learn new things about themselves and the change they're facing, and that that will help them as they continue to deal with the transition process once the workshop is over.

The other goal is that participants will learn more about change and how to deal with it, in general, which they can then apply to future changes in their lives.

Activity 5: Feedback (20 minutes)

Next, ask everyone to share the change they've chosen. Ask each participant to explain to the group what change they'll be working on, what transition stage they think they are in, and how they are feeling about the transition process right now. Group members may ask questions or provide supportive feedback.

Closing Reflection (5 minutes)

Direct teens to the Closing Reflection section of their journals.

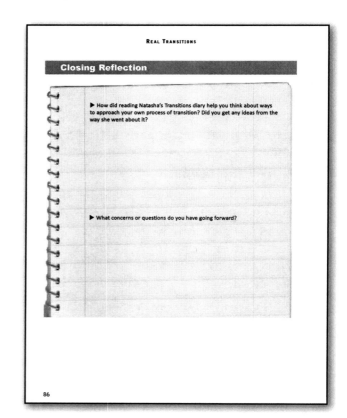

REAL TRANSITIONS

Closing Reflection

▶ How did reading Natasha's Transitions diary help you think about ways to approach your own process of transition? Did you get any ideas from the way she went about it?

▶ What concerns or questions do you have going forward?

86

School Daze
I tried to change my old ways at a new school

Natasha Santos

By Natasha Santos

So there I was on the train to visit City-As-School for the first time. From what I'd been told, it was an alternative high school for people who don't feel comfortable in a traditional school setting. Translation: Some rinky-dink hole-in-the-wall manufactured to house academic misfits. But I was failing at my old school, so I didn't have much choice.

My mother's death, "growing pains," a creeping sense of failure and an inability to communicate what help I needed had all contributed to me not doing well in school.

In therapy, I was working out many of the painful feelings and events of my childhood that I'd tried to suppress for years. Dealing with awful feelings that I'd never dealt with before took its toll on my motivation and then my grades.

Sitting in the City-As auditorium, I told myself I was too smart for this. Sure I had failed, but I would do better. My mind began to change as I heard the assistant principal say something like, "It is your responsibility to take control of your education. We'll help you if that's what you want. The traditional public school system wasn't good enough for you so you sought out an alternative. You haven't been accepted yet, but you have made the first step."

Two weeks later I registered for classes. Unlike most schools, at City-As students get most of their credits through internships. For science credit, I started working at the Central Park Zoo.

I found my classes and internships engaging. I also liked that teachers didn't give much homework. But at the same time I felt—and still feel—that I hadn't been through a process of transition to really feeling like I could succeed in school and that I was on the right path to adulthood.

When I signed up for the Transitions workshop, I decided to focus on making that change. In the group, we tried specific activities (we called them "tools") that we thought would help us make a change in our lives, and we kept journals of our efforts. Here's my journal of my attempts to succeed in my new school and be in charge of my education and future.

Session 1

At my old school, Murrow, I didn't have too much trouble with the workload. My real problem was feeling disconnected—I felt like a loner.

When I first entered Murrow (as a sophomore, transferring from a smaller school) I wasn't brave enough to connect with other students. Then, as I felt more and more lonely, I didn't spend enough time actually at school to meet people. I've decided that at City-As I need to actually show up, and be brave enough to put myself out there. (Gulp.)

It's always been easier for me to connect with adults than with people my age, so for my first challenge, I decided to speak to teachers about the change I am trying to make and ask their advice about how to succeed.

I loved this tool! I got nothing but positivity from my teachers. When I asked my social studies teacher how I was doing he said, "Great, you're one of the most involved and mature people in my class."

And my English teacher seemed enraptured by my work. It was a nice break from Murrow where I was constantly avoiding teachers because I had cut their class and had work due. Perhaps my family was right— I just needed to leave Murrow and start fresh to succeed.

Session 2

One tool is to write letters to people you are or have been close to, even if you don't send them. I decided to write a letter to Murrow telling the school why I'm making this change, and saying good-bye. I decided to keep my letter short and sweet because I didn't want to cry or shout or go completely crazy. I wrote:

Dear Murrow,

I came to Murrow to get what I had always wanted: a place where I was welcomed and academically challenged. I also had always wanted to feel connected to school and the people there (maybe because I felt so disconnected in my foster home).

School had never been a problem for me in the past. I would never have been voted Ms. Popular, but I knew who I was through my academics. I was an overachiever. People called me weird and unique and smart.

That has been part of my persona since elementary school. My home life was always crazy, so school was the place that anchored me to a reality that I wanted. All of this was possible as long as I stayed the smart, dependable student. No matter what else I may have been, I was always that.

When I started failing in Murrow I could no longer identify myself as the achiever and the smart one. Smart ones didn't fail classes. Overachievers achieved with ease. I was still the weird one, but even that took on a kind of melancholy tilt.

Now I am going to try to find a new me in a new school.

Wish me luck,

Tasha

I think writing the letter helped me understand more of what had happened. But when I looked back at it a few weeks later, I didn't feel released: I felt upset and disappointed in Murrow and myself. I guess it was time to begin feeling some of the emotions I wouldn't let myself feel while I was still at Murrow.

Session 3

This week I decided to talk to some of the people who I thought were interesting and nice in my English class.

I expected it to be easy to work on my social skills and my feelings of belonging. But trying to make friends also brought up some feelings from my past that I didn't expect. In my other schools and foster homes I had always had trouble with fitting in and belonging. I was rejected by some of my former classmates and my former foster mother after I gave so much of myself.

Talking to my classmates, I noticed I was anxious about putting myself out there. I felt afraid that there was something wrong with me, something unlovable and unchangeable that made everyone run away and will make anyone new run away, too.

I did meet one guy named Jess who was real cool. He has blue hair and a constant nervous smile. He first caught my attention because he was good at math (I'm terrible at math). I decided to ask Jess for help (really I just copied his answers, but it was a start).

Now that I've talked to him, I have someone to call about homework and maybe become friends with.

I feel pretty proud that I was brave enough to put myself out there and try to get to know someone.

Session 4

I decided to speak to three new people a day at my school. I thought that talking to people would be just like a ritual, and would become more and more comfortable. But it went terribly. I found out just how big of a coward I am about meeting people. At best I would say, "Hi, how are you doing," to two people. At worst I would just smile and nod to everyone I saw.

I thought that I would become outgoing, the center of attention, just because I wanted to. I guess I'm more reserved than I knew. I feel pretty bad about the whole thing. I feel like I found out I am a big 'fraidy cat and that no one in my new school really wants to get to know me.

It reminded me of what happened at Murrow. Murrow seemed like the perfect climate for me at first. It was open and intellectual: there were hundreds of groups and cliques and tons of clubs to join. But instead of finding a way to join a single group, I became a loner and recluse. In a building with thousands of people, I was alone.

At other times, when I'd experienced this failure to connect, I'd never blamed it on myself. I'd blamed it on my foster mother, my social workers and the kids at my previous stupid narrow-minded school. But if it still happened in a place like Murrow, the only person I could really blame was myself, and that hurt. Trying to meet people at City-As, I wondered if it could happen again, and if something terrible was wrong with me.

After two weeks of trying, I decided I was putting myself out there more than I wanted to and it brought up too many old feelings of rejection that I don't want to deal with.

Session 5

In the workshop this week, I didn't talk about how hard my last two weeks were, and how I felt like giving up. I don't think anyone noticed, but I felt bad after the meeting. I felt like I was lying in a place where everyone had agreed to be as open and honest as possible.

For my tool this week I decided not to try anything that would require interacting with new people. Instead, I chose to write in my diary about my school life. It didn't go well. Some days I would open up my journal and think of all the things I should write, and other days I just would stare at it in its place on the headboard in my room.

In the end, I was too afraid to actually record what I had felt and experienced during the day. So I changed my tool. I took some time out each day to go bike riding. I've just learned to ride a bike (late bloomer) and I love this new ability of mine. While I'm riding I just have my thoughts and the feeling of riding through the wind. (Though I should also try to pay a little attention to the bike and the road—I fell off three times.) If I couldn't face my feelings, at least I could escape them for a while.

Session 6

The workshop is almost over, so I decided to hold a "Congratulations on Our Successful Transitions" luncheon. I planned on inviting all the participants in the workshop.

I made out invitations, but then I realized that I didn't feel all that successful, so celebrating didn't feel honest to me. In fact, I was feeling even more like I was only faking my transition. I didn't even try to do my tools during the last two weeks.

Looking Back

Later, looking over my transitions diary, I realized that this pattern is familiar to me: I tend to come out strong, then get scared and back away. I've been trying to be a person I'm not comfortable being and to enjoy experiences I can't really handle.

I realized that I want to take things slower, not expecting to make 10 new best friends in two weeks, but just to find one or two people to talk to about our classes, little things like that. I want to evaluate my goals and how to achieve them without overwhelming myself.

If I'm reasonable about what I expect from myself, I think I might accomplish much more. In fact, lately I've been feeling less overwhelmed and isolated at school. I'm participating in my classes, my grades are good, and I'm slowly meeting my classmates. I might actually have some good experiences in high school after all.

Even though I don't yet feel connected to my school and fully responsible for my education and life, I think the tools have helped me better understand the process of transition.

Before, I saw changes as things that happen to you whether you're ready or not. I didn't see changes as opening up the possibility of internal development. And I've always been afraid that I don't have what it takes to make any change, whatever it is.

I realize now that my life will be a continuing cycle of transitions, and that the changes I need to make can help me grow, not leave me stuck further and further behind. I also see that I try to make changes happen too quickly. Now I see that I can slow down. That makes me feel more confident in my ability to evolve and grow.

Session 9: Tools That Will Work for Me

Workshop Summary

Teens will develop a plan for choosing and using tools to apply to their chosen change.

Time: 2 hours

Materials: Teen Journal and Leader's Guide, toolboxes (from Session 4)

Goals:

1. Teens will set goals and make a plan for reaching those goals.
2. Teens will explore and review the benefits of sharing with the group, and think about how to set appropriate boundaries for their own sharing.

Activity 1: M&Ms Check-In (10 minutes)

See description in Session 3.

Activity 2: Personal Ground Rules (20 minutes)

 Tell the teens:

This half of our workshop is going to look and feel different from the first half. You'll be working on your own change and transition process directly by trying out different tools each week, and reporting back to the group about how it went.

We'll be doing a lot of sharing through our transition process, and sometimes it may get very emotional, because transitions are tough.

We're going to start off today with two activities that can help you think a little bit more about how to manage the next six weeks—setting personal ground rules for yourself, and setting boundaries on what you want to share or not share.

• Direct teens to the "Personal Ground Rules" page in their journals (p. 88) and read the instructions aloud together.

• Explain that this activity will help them anticipate what might be difficult about this half of the workshop, and strategize a few ways to deal with that. It can be particularly helpful for people who have a hard time staying motivated or who tend to become overwhelmed by new projects.

• Give teens about 15 minutes to write their ground rules. Then ask for a few volunteers to

Personal Ground Rules

As we've seen already, the workshop can sometimes make us feel great. Other times it can raise difficult emotions that we don't know how to deal with. The following list can help you focus on issues that may come up for you as we proceed through the second half of the transitions workshop. We've already created some ground rules for the group. After you become conscious of how you respond to difficult emotions, you can create some personal ground rules, to help yourself deal with those difficult moments if they arise.

Check off any of the sentences that apply to you. Feel free to add others:

☐ I usually go further than I'm really comfortable going and then feel burnt out.

☐ I often put too much pressure on myself to succeed, and wind up feeling like I'm failing.

☐ I can feel so afraid of trying, that I don't try at all.

☐ I know I'll beat myself up for not using my tools right.

☐ I'm afraid this workshop will bring up strong emotions and I'll freak out.

☐ I'm afraid I'll stir up bad feelings and then be all alone with them.

☐ When things get hard, I withdraw and go through the motions without paying attention to what I'm really feeling or really letting people know what I'm struggling with.

☐ When things get hard I'm afraid I'll skip sessions without paying attention to what I'm struggling with.

☐ I'm afraid I'll quit when I get uncomfortable.

☐ _____

☐ _____

☐ _____

☐ _____

Adapted from *The Courage to Heal Workbook* by Laura Davis

88

Session 9: Tools That Will Work for Me

Now use the issues you've identified as the basis for your ground rules.

For example, if you push yourself too hard and then feel burnt out, you might want to limit the amount of time you'll devote to using your tools. If you're so afraid of trying that you never start, you might want to give yourself a specific time to devote to using your tools each week, even if you hate every minute and your efforts feel like a total flop.

Don't write down any ground rules that feel forced. Your ground rules should be things that you think will work for you.

Take a few minutes to write down some beginning ground rules here:

89

share their responses. (If nobody wants to share, that's OK.)

Activity 3: Setting Boundaries for Sharing With the Group (15 minutes)

• Direct teens to the "Setting Boundaries" worksheet (p. 90) and read through it together. This activity is important in making teens self-aware of how much they are comfortable sharing with the group.

Explain to the teens that it's important that they feel a sense of control over how much they share, and this activity will help them think about that. Give them 10 minutes or so to complete the activity.

Activity 4: Choosing A Tool (20 minutes)

• Next, explain to teens that they'll choose one main tool to focus on each week for the next six weeks. Pass back the toolboxes they made in Session 4, and tell them that they can look

through these, as well as at their Personal Tool Banks and the Tools Cheat Sheet from their journals, to find a tool they'd like to try out this week.

Tell the teens that once they have selected their tool, they should fill out the "Choosing a Tool" page in their journals (p. 91). Explain that they'll be completing this sheet every week and will use it to map out what they plan to try in the week ahead.

Activity 5: Sharing Your Tool (45 minutes)

• Explain to the group that each week, they'll share with each other the tools they're going to try out. By talking through their plans with the group, members can help each other refine their tools and think about potential challenges. (This is a good time to remind everyone of the difference between support and advice.)

• Go around the room and ask each teen to share which tool they are going to try this week. They can read/summarize as much or as little of

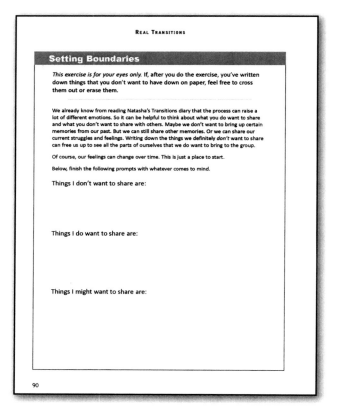

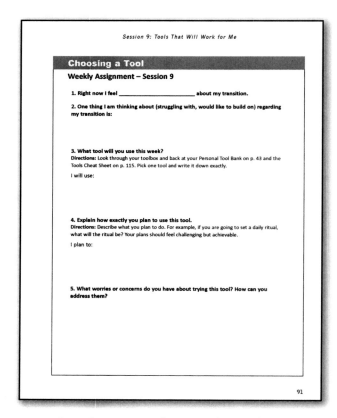

what they wrote on their worksheet as they like.

They should give the group a clear idea of exactly what they'll be doing. (e.g., if someone says they are going to "reconnect with friends" this week, ask if they have a more specific idea of how they're going to do that—will they call or email an old friend? Make plans to hang out with someone they haven't seen lately? Make a point of talking with a new friend? Etc.) Allow a few minutes for each teen to discuss their tool and get feedback from you and the group.

Note: Here and every week during the tool review, make sure to note if a tool seems too difficult or if a teen seems unaware of the potential consequences. (Often other teens in your group will point this out.)

For example, if a teen says he is going to confront a parent about not being around for him as a child, try to help him think through what he's hoping to get from that conversation and if he'd be able to deal with the parent not responding the way he'd like them to.

Likewise, notice if a teen seems to be avoiding trying any significant tools, or if they use the same kind of tool

every week, and encourage them to take a risk or branch out.

Closing Reflection (10 minutes)

Direct teens to complete the closing reflection sheet for this session.

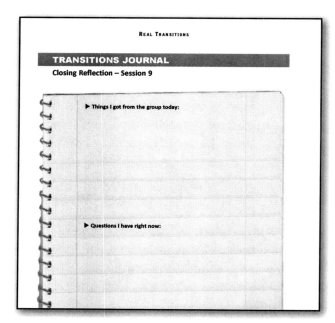

Sessions 10-15: Using the Tools

Workshop Summary

Teens will try out different tools to apply to their chosen change.

Time: 2 hours

Materials: Teen Journal and Leader's Guide, toolboxes

Goals:

1. Teens will put the tools and their understanding of the Transitions process into practice as they work on a transition.
2. Teens will continue building trust and supportive communication skills as they discuss their progress with the group.

Note: Use this format for each of the next six sessions. Each week, teens will report back on the tool they tried last week and pick a new tool for the week ahead.

In week 15, instead of picking new tools, participants will reflect on the work they've done over the course of the workshop.

Because each session begins by asking the teens to report back on their tools, we've omitted the M&M check-in. However, if this worked well for your teens, feel free to include a modified version or an alternate opening ritual or icebreaker.

Activity 1: Transitions Journal— Reporting Back (60 minutes)

• Direct teens to complete the "Reporting Back" worksheet (15 minutes).

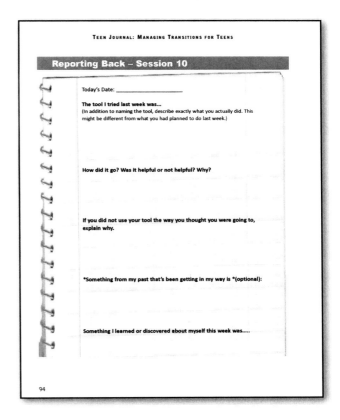

Note: The first time you do this activity, emphasize that it's important for everyone to be honest in their report backs. Tell the teens that there may be weeks when they didn't do the tool they said they were going to do, for whatever reason, or when the tool they tried didn't work out. That's OK.

What's most important is that everyone is honest in reflecting on what happened. If they didn't do a tool this week, or if they did something different—why? That's what they should write and talk about. (Are they feeling overwhelmed? Did the tool seem too hard? Are they feeling bored or stuck? These are all important things to note and explore with the group).

• Next, have teens share out their responses with the group (45 minutes) and invite group members to respond, using support prompts/questioning techniques learned and practiced in prior workshop sessions. (If teens can't recall the prompts and techniques, refer back to p. 24 in their journals.)

Activity 2: Choosing and Sharing a Tool (50 minutes)

• Hand out toolboxes. Direct teens to the worksheet "Choosing a Tool" and have them fill it out, just like they did last week. Give them about 20 minutes to choose a tool and complete the worksheet, then ask everyone to share their chosen tool with the group. Remind the group that their role is to ask questions and provide feedback to make sure everyone has a clear plan for the week ahead. Remember that it's also your role to make sure teens are using appropriate tools—trying new things while maintaining realistic expectations for themselves.

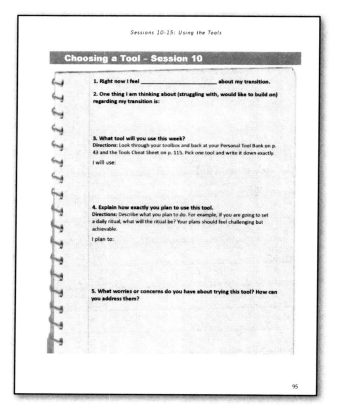

Note: In week 15, the last session before the celebration, teens will not choose another tool to work on. Instead, you can use this time to ask teens to write a brief reflection on how the past six weeks have gone, where they are with their transitions now, and what they'd like to continue to work on beyond the workshop. Ask for volunteers to share some of their thoughts on what has been learned and what the group as a whole has accomplished. What did people find most challenging? What was helpful? Etc. You may also want to set aside some time during Session 15 to plan for the graduation/celebration the following week.

Closing Reflection (10 minutes)

Direct teens to complete the closing reflection sheet for this session.

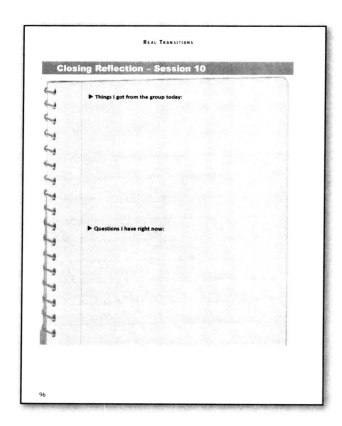

Session 16: Celebrating Our Accomplishments

Session 16 is a chance to mark the progress that teens have made over the course of the workshop by doing something ceremonial, such as a graduation, fun group outing, or other event. It's ideal to include the teens in the planning process so that they have something to look forward to even though the workshop is ending. (Involving them in the planning process will also help them feel more in control of this ending.)

This is a celebration, not a lesson, so we have not included a set of procedures. But it is essential to acknowledge, both during today's workshop and in the weeks leading up to it, what the group is gaining and losing as we say goodbye to one another (goodbye, at least, in the context of the Transitions workshop).

We suggest that you include in today's session ample space for sharing, such as a longer check-in, so that everyone has a chance to speak about the feelings they have about moving on and saying goodbye to the group. For example,

 Say (in your own words):

Our group is approaching the end of a very powerful shared experience, and we are about to encounter a change in that we'll no longer be meeting as a group. That's prompting us to enter yet another process of transition, and we're likely to cycle now through the stages we've all become so familiar with: Letting Go, Chaos, and New Start. Many of you have already begun that process.

At the same time, we are here today to celebrate the great things we've gained through this experience: new friends, a better understanding of ourselves and others, and a great set of tools we can use now and throughout our lives to cope with

change and keep moving toward our goals.

So let's take some time to check in with one another and reflect on how we're feeling, and what we've gained these many weeks we've spent together.

Thoughts on organizing your closing ceremonies

Aside from the check-in, the format for today's session is up to you and your teens. But we have included a description of some of the things we did as part of our Transitions "Graduation." Try any of these that seem useful, and feel free to add your own creative ideas! The point is to positively acknowledge each participant and what they've accomplished, remind them to keep using the knowledge and tools they've developed in the workshop, and affirm that the group members can continue to support each other even without the structure of a group.

• Letter-writing activity: Give teens about 20 minutes to write a letter to their future selves. Tell them that the letters should be opened a year from now, and ask them to think about where they'd like to be at that point in time.

For guidance, write the following questions on the board:

In one year...

Where do you hope you'll be with your transition?

How would you like to be handling any future changes that might come along?

What have you learned and accomplished here that you'd like to remind your future selves about?

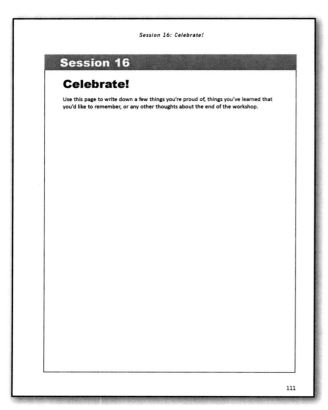

- Buy teens scrapbooks or journals as gifts to encourage further self-expression.

- Make a list of everyone's contact information and encourage them to stay in touch and think of each other as part of their support system in the future.

- Serve a cake or cupcakes with a candle for each participant to set an intention on and blow out.

- If your program budget allows, take teens out for a meal at a restaurant, visit a museum, go bowling, go to a ropes course, or some other fun group activity.

(If you feel confident that you will be in touch with the teens in a year, you can collect the letters and mail them at the appropriate time. Otherwise, ask teens to seal their letters and address them with the date they should be opened.)

- Make official-looking "diplomas" on the computer on cardstock paper (or buy some nice-looking certificates and print the relevant information on them). Then write a personal letter to each teen, focusing on their strengths, growth, and accomplishments during the workshop.

As you present each diploma, read the letter (or a few excerpts) to convey how much each teen has grown and developed during the workshop.

- Take a group photo at some point in the workshop and make copies to present to each teen (we found reasonably-priced frames for the photos and they made very attractive gifts that remind everyone of the group's unity and support).

APPENDIX

ALTERNATE LESSON FOR SESSION 5
TEN TIPS & TRICKS FOR LEADING GROUPS
FACILITATION TROUBLESHOOTING

Alternate Lesson for Letting Go (Session 5)

If you'd like to do more reading in your group, use this activity in place of, or in addition to, the Timeline of My Life activity in Session 5.

Learning How to Let Go (75 minutes)

• Direct teens to the "Learning How to Let Go" worksheet in their journals (p. 149). Read aloud the first page.

• Depending on the size of your group, divide teens into partners or small teams.

• Explain that each pair/team will read a different story that shows the writer going through the experience of Letting Go, in very different ways. Then, they'll analyze what they read on the accompanying worksheet and report back to the whole group.

• Assign each team/pair a story. The stories and their themes are:

"Letting Go," by Cynthia Orbes (death of a parent)

"Starting Over Without Them," by H. R. (parental addiction and mental illness)

"Taking Myself to Anger School," by Eric Green (childhood abuse/neglect)

Tell them to take turns reading aloud in their groups. (25 minutes)

• Next, direct them to discuss and complete the questions on the worksheet together. (25 minutes) Circulate around the room to make sure teens are on the right track, and encourage them to think deeply. Ask questions and offer hints if groups are stuck.

• Finally, call everyone back together and ask each group to share their assigned story and responses. (25 minutes)

Alternate Lesson for Letting Go (Session 5)

Following is another activity to learn about the Letting Go stage. It involves reading one of the following three stories, which were all written by teens who were struggling with loss, and thinking about the questions on this worksheet with a partner or in a small group. You may or may not use this lesson in your workshop. If you don't, feel free to read the stories on your own—they can help you reflect on the difficulties of letting go, and how to find ways to move forward.

Learning How to Let Go

After your team takes turns reading aloud the assigned story, discuss and answer together the following questions.

Story title: _____

Author: _____

1. Describe the transition that the writer is going through: What was the big change s/he went through, and what is the change s/he is trying to make?

2. What is the writer losing (good or bad) in this transition?

3. What is hard for the writer about letting go? What prevents him/her from letting go, and how does being stuck in the Letting Go stage affect him/her?

4. Thinking about your toolkit, what tools do you think would be most helpful to the writer in finding his/her way through the Letting Go stage? Why?

Ten Tips and Tricks for Leading Groups

1. Keep a log of every youth you work with. After each session, spend a few moments and write a couple of sentences about what has stood out for you about each student in the group. Include your concerns, but *always* write at least one sentence on what you like about this young person or a positive quality they have. This is *especially* important for young people who get under your skin. If you consciously and explicitly write about a positive side or strength in their personality or behavior, that insight will start to seep into your interactions with them, and it will make a huge difference to you, to them, and to your group (see tip #5).

Review your log right before the next session, at least until you feel you have gotten to know the students well.

2. Build and maintain trust by recognizing young people for their contributions. Remember: young people *crave* recognition and *hate* humiliation (just like the rest of us, only more so). When students deserve recognition, give it freely.

Be affirming. In many discussions, you will find students making thoughtful or creative contributions that never occurred to you. Reflect those contributions back to them. Let them know that when they put their minds to something (such as a problem with a supervisor, or a conflict with a roommate) they may know even better than adults how to solve it.

Give special roles. The activities in this guide provide opportunities to give students special "jobs" that allow them to contribute and to see their contributions recognized (for example, recording responses on chart paper or being a group spokesperson). This can be particularly useful if you have a student who is disruptive, to help refocus his or her energy in a more positive direction. Remember that "troublemakers" are often leaders in disguise.

Giving them a role, such as leading an activity with you, can tap their leadership skills, and put *them* in the position of managing group behavior.

3. Build and maintain trust by managing conflicts respectfully. If a student does something in the session that requires a reprimand, calmly note the inappropriate activity (so the other know that you won't let it slide), but talk to the student privately, after class, about the specifics. For minor misbehaviors and acting out, remind everyone about the group guidelines and expectations instead of singling a student out. For example, "Remember, when everyone speaks at the same time, it's difficult to hear what anyone has to say, so let's try to keep to our 'one mic' rule."

Ask, Don't Tell: When talking to students about a conflict, ask students what happened, their perception of why it happened, how they feel about it, and how they can use that information next time or to solve the problem now.

For example: "Why do you think that person was upset about the comment you made during group? What could you do differently next time?"

4. Don't feel you have to know everything or solve every problem. As the facilitator, it's your job to keep the group safe: to set an appropriate tone, to pay attention to potential conflicts and respond to them quickly and appropriately, and to help keep group discussions constructive.

But it's also important to remember that the teens in your group are the experts on their own lives. When the group is discussing how to deal with a challenging situation, like the losses experience by Griffin Kinard in Session 2, you simply cannot assume you know the answer (or even what the problem is). Make sure you allow space for them to express what they know, and respect their views even when they differ from your own.

That can feel disconcerting, but as you get comfortable, it can also be very exciting. If students see that you take delight in learning from them and in their often-creative responses to the challenges they face, you will actually have more influence with them.

5. Monitor your reactions to the most difficult students.
How you respond to the difficult students can set a tone for the entire class. Students will watch your interactions with their peers very closely in deciding how to behave themselves—including how supportive they will be toward you.

When you begin working with a new group, it is worth devoting extra time and energy early on to thinking about how to respond to the most challenging students. Your skill and compassion in handling them and setting boundaries for them is a litmus test for the other young people: the better you perform, the more they will trust and respect you.

6. Be nonjudgmental.
Nothing will cause young people to clam up faster than the feeling that they are being judged. For example, if students describe outrageous behavior, don't common on the behavior. Instead, ask what they learned from it. Here are two strategies for being nonjudgmental:

Trust in the values in the stories and the activities. Youth Communication stories are carefully designed to promote positive values. However, they also acknowledge negative values and bad choices, so those may come up in conversation. Our experience in teaching hundreds of stories is that the good values win out in the end. So don't get freaked out if some negative ideas pop up early in the story or in discussion. They will get resolved by the end.

Use the power of the group. If one student makes an outrageous comment, instead of reprimanding him, ask mildly, "Does anyone else have another opinion on this topic?" Nine times out of 10, another student will present a contrary view—which will be much more powerful than your doing so.

7. Show that you're listening to and aware of everyone in the group.
When participants are speaking, make eye contact, don't interrupt, and give signs of listening like nodding and using encouraging phrases such as "uh-huh" and "yeah." Also, make sure you understand what someone is feeling and saying by restating comments (paraphrasing) or asking for clarification.

Stacking: When several participants wish to speak at once, it is useful to "stack" them by simply calling on one participant and then saying who will speak next and who will speak after that. When people know their desire to participate has been acknowledged, they can relax and listen while they wait their turn.

8. Avoid the veiled quiz.
When you are leading discussions, you want to avoid the "veiled quiz." The veiled quiz is asking a question that you already know the answer to, getting a response from teens, and pretending that it's a discussion.

The veiled quiz is common in school, where teachers want to check in with students to see if they have learned the material. There's nothing wrong with it as long as it doesn't masquerade as a real discussion. But in the *Managing Transitions for Teens* program, the goal is to spark a discussion—to get the teens engaged—not to quiz teens on what they know.

Veiled quiz questions tend to have answers that are either correct or incorrect. They feel like school, and in an out-of-school-time setting, they can shut down discussion. Instead, try asking open-ended questions that encourage participants to think about how they feel about the issues raised in the story or activity, or how the ideas relate to their own lives.

9. Challenge teens to think deeply. After asking a question of the group, wait several seconds before accepting answers: this eliminates competition to be first with an answer and allows all participants to assimilate the question and consider a response. For those times when participants are reluctant to speak, waiting patiently is more useful than filling the silence with the sound of your own voice.

Ask follow-up questions. You can also help participants explore and expand their ideas and feelings by asking open-ended follow-up questions. Follow-up questions can ask participants to give examples of personal stories that illuminate the topic under discussion, and to compare and connect ideas, or simply say a little more about the topic.

Play devil's advocate. Don't be afraid to raise issues that are contrary to what you or your students might expect (even unpopular or "politically incorrect" views). This helps the group consider more options, and it helps you avoid being pigeonholed as someone who always responds in a predictable way.

10. Go with the flow (within reason). The lessons in the manual provide a framework for helping young people explore their lives and imagine constructive solutions to their challenges. During the first half of the workshop series, lessons are sequenced so that teens understand the major concepts of change and transition, are able to organize a transition into three major stages, and learn "tools," or coping mechanisms, they can use to manage a transition at each stage. But unlike academic lessons, you do not necessarily have to complete all of these exactly as written to be successful.

If teens are particularly engaged with an activity or discussion (or upset or confused about it) you can allow more time to explore it, even if that means having to condense or eliminate something else. As long as you see that teens are grasping the major concepts and able to apply them, it's OK to go with

the flow and adapt the curriculum to meet the needs of your group.

But also remember that the work of transitions is hard, the teens may simply want to avoid doing it. It's a judgment call. You can allow for some wandering off the path of the planned discussion, but you need to get back to it before too long or you'll never reach the destination.

Facilitation Troubleshooting

PROBLEM	ASK YOURSELF...	TRY...
Everybody talking	Is it because they're so interested?	Ask them to tell their idea to a partner.
	Is it because they are *not* interested?	Rephrase the question, or add interest to the topic, or drop it.
	Is it because they have not heard the topic?	Get their attention first, check your timing, review the ground rules, etc.
Nobody talking	Do they understand?	Rephrase the question. Give more information.
	Are they interested?	Clarify the topic or question and challenge them to consider it.
	Do they need to think more to formulate their ideas?	Wait! Give them time to think. You may also invite them to discuss the question with a partner or write individually about it.
	Are they comfortable?	Help them get to know you and each other better by playing icebreaker games.
Side conversations or interference	Is the discussion hitting too close to home?	Give participants time to write individually about the topic, or table the discussion. Remind teens they don't have to reveal personal information.
	Is the discussion of no concern to them?	Acknowledge the fact, and shorten the meeting if possible.
Shocking or "funny" statements	Is it really in order to get attention? Or could it be a method to cover up feeling embarrassed?	Deal with this directly. Keep your sense of humor! Sometimes you may decide to have a private talk with the individual(s) involved, particularly if this is a pattern.
	Is it from an inability to express themselves clearly?	Rephrase by asking, "Do you mean...?" Or ask them to rephrase—and give them some time.
Someone too disruptive to stay in the group	How can I stop the behavior and not build resentment? How can I help the person take responsibility for his or her own behavior?	Ask the person to leave the group until she or he is able to return without being disruptive. Consider giving the person a leadership role.

Some of the ideas in this section are adapted from *Ways We Want Our Class To Be*, a publication of the Developmental Studies Center (Oakland, CA, 1996).

About the Writers and Editors

Autumn Spanne is the editor of *Represent*, Youth Communication's national magazine by and for youth in foster care. Prior to working at Youth Communication, Autumn was a reporter for newspapers in Massachusetts and California and spent five years teaching English and journalism on the Navajo Nation. She has a BA in literature from the University of California, Santa Cruz, an MS in journalism from Columbia University, and an MA in education from Western New Mexico University.

Rachel Blustain edited Youth Communication's two teen magazines, *Represent* and *New Youth Connections* for several years. She has worked as a reporter and freelance writer for many publications, including a stint as the Moscow reporter for the *Forward*. She has a BA from Brown University and an MSW from the Hunter College (CUNY) School of Social Work.

Laura Longhine is the editorial director at Youth Communication. She edited the foster teen magazine *Represent* for three years, and has edited numerous Youth Communication books and curricula covering social-emotional topics for teens. She has a BA in English from Tufts University and an MS in journalism from Columbia University.

Nora McCarthy edited Youth Communication's two teen magazines: *Represent* and *New Youth Connections*. In 2005, she founded Rise (risemagazine.org), a nonprofit that trains parents to write about their experiences with the child welfare system in order to support parents and parent advocacy and guide child welfare practitioners and policymakers in becoming more responsive to the families and communities they serve. She is a graduate of the Medill School of Journalism at Northwestern University.

Keith Hefner co-founded Youth Communication in 1980 and has directed it ever since. He is the recipient of the Luther P. Jackson Education Award from the New York Association of Black Journalists and a MacArthur Fellowship. He was also a Revson Fellow at Columbia University. He has written and tested curriculum that accompanies Youth Communication's teen-written books and magazines for more than 20 years.

Read. Write. Succeed.

About Youth Communication

Youth Communication, founded in 1980, is nonprofit educational publishing company located in New York City. Our mission is to help marginalized youth develop their full potential through reading and writing, so that they can succeed in school and at work and contribute to their communities.

Youth Communication publishes true stories by teens that are developed in a rigorous writing program. We offer more than 50 books that adults can use to engage reluctant teen readers on an array of topics including peer pressure, school, sex, and relationships. Our stories also appear in our two award-winning magazines, *YCteen* and *Represent*, and on our website (www.youthcomm.org), and are frequently reprinted in popular and professional magazines and textbooks. We offer hundreds of lessons, complete leader's guides (like this one), and professional development to guide educators in using the stories to help teens improve their academic, social, and emotional skills.

Our stories, written by a diverse group of writers, are uniquely compelling to peers who do not see their experiences reflected in mainstream reading materials. They motivate teens to read and write, encourage good values, and show teens how to make positive changes in their lives.

You can access many of our stories and sample lessons for free at www.youthcomm.org. For more information on our products and services, contact Loretta Chan at 212-279-0708 x115, or lchan@youthcomm.org.

Youth Communication®
224 W. 29th St, 2nd Fl.
New York, NY 10001
212-279-0708
www.youthcomm.org

Managing Transitions Resource Guide

There are several other excellent transitions resources for working with youth in foster care which you may want to consider using with teens in your groups. Here are brief descriptions of five of them.

Transitioning From Foster Care: An Experiential Activity Guidebook

Institute for Public Sector Innovation of the Muskie School of Public Service, University of Southern Maine.

This guidebook is an essential resource for experiential activities that help youth understand and apply the Transition framework to their lives. With fun physical challenges and art activities that were shaped by youth, these activities create a non-threatening environment for youth to begin reflecting on significant change that they have experienced.

Inside Out Cards

Created by A Home Within
www.ahomewithin.org

This deck of 16 cards prompts youth to reflect on significant changes that they have experienced and offers activities that help them manage the transition. Each card relates to a different Transition phase and helps youth explore how change engages the mind, body, heart, and soul.

The deck can be used with individual youth or to guide a series of group sessions. Download pdfs of the cards at www.fosteringtransitions.org. The website also provides ideas for how to use the cards and additional case studies that reinforce transitions concepts.

A Home Within has also created *Outside In* cards specifically for pregnant and parenting youth.

Flux

Created by the Foster Care Alumni Association
www.FosterCareAlumni.org/FLUX

With powerful stories, artwork, guidance and support from more than 100 alumni, FLUX was written to support young people in the emotional transition from foster care to adulthood. FLUX offers honest, useful, and juicy real-life expertise that can only come from those who have experienced the system first-hand.

The authors meaningfully apply Transitions concepts to birth family relationships, building support systems, parenting, and intimacy topics. This is not a facilitation guide, but because it offers reflection questions and suggested activities for each phase of Transition and touches on a range of topics, it is an invaluable tool for shaping a group workshop or individual consultations with youth.

FLUX is available for purchase at www.fostercarealumni.org/FLUX for $15.99. FCAA also offers FLUX training led by foster care alumni, which is suited for youth ages 16 – 24.

The book includes facilitator notes, lists of materials, and step-by-step instructions for carrying out the activities and guiding reflection. Activities can be carried out in an ongoing series of workshops or can be used individually to enhance existing programs – there are some great ideas for icebreakers!

Copies of the book can be downloaded from: www.transitionandsocialchange.org.

Bridges to Independence
**Walden Family Services,
San Diego, CA**

This is a ten-session curriculum for guiding teens in foster care through the transition of leaving the system and preparing for life on their own. The program provides a thorough examination of Transition and applies the concepts to the multitude of changes that youth face in preparing to exit the system. It includes journaling exercises, art projects, experiential activities, and games.

To download a copy of the Facilitator Guide and Participant Workbook, visit: www.transitionandsocialchange.org.

MORE RESOURCES ON THE WEB

The **Transitions Knowledge Bank** (www.transitionandsocialchange. org) contains a **Resource** section that includes several individual activities for managing each phase of Transition. Exercises are organized by the key pillars that guide the process of navigating each phase.

These are general exercises that can be used one-on-one with youth or incorporated into ongoing group workshops. They are broad enough to be used in a range of contexts and to allow each organization to customize them to their youth population.

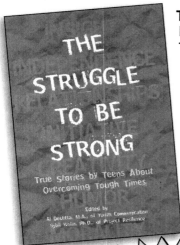

MANAGING TRANSITIONS FOR TEENS

FOR TEENS

Teen Journal: Managing Transitions for Teens

Book, 178 pp., ISBN #9781935552727, $12.95*

This Teen Journal (and the whole Transitions program) can help you learn how to manage transitions in your life, so you can take more control over what's happening. You'll learn about the stages people go through when they're facing a change, and try out lots of strategies to make the process easier. When you finish the workshop, this journal will be a record of everything you've accomplished, and a blueprint you can use to help you handle transitions in the future.

eader's Guide to naging Transitions for ns

, 122 pp.,
N #9781935552710, $16.95*

16 sessions, you'll engage teens arning about the different stages ansition and the tools they can o cope. And you'll help them y those tools to a real transi- they are trying to make in their . The strategies they learn in this s op will help them in all of the re changes they face, from leaving ystem to moving to new jobs, es, or relationships.

FOR TEACHERS & STAFF

ad. Write. Succeed.

Return order form to: Youth Communication, 224 W. 29th St., 2nd fl., New York, NY 10001, Tel: 212-279-0708 x. 115, FAX 212-279-8856

Order online today at: www.youthcomm.org

CPSIA information can be obtained
at www.ICGtesting.com
Printed in the USA
FFOW02n1734031014
7781FF